SS UNITED STATES

SPEED QUEEN OF THE SEAS

SS UNITED STATES

SPEED QUEEN OF THE SEAS

WILLIAM H. MILLER

AMBERLEY

This book is dedicated to all the crewmembers of the United States Merchant Marine

Cover illustrations by William G. Muller (www.williamgmuller.com)

First published 2009
Amberley Publishing
Cirencester Road, Chalford,
Stroud, Gloucestershire, GL6 8PE

www.amberley-books.com

British Library Cataloguing in Publication Data.
A catalogue record for this book is available from the British Library.

ISBN 978 1 84868 365 5

Typesetting and origination by **FonthillMedia**
Printed in Great Britain

CONTENTS

ACKNOWLEDGEMENTS

As in manning a great ship such as the *United States*, many have served in the creation and preparation of this book. First, my deep appreciation to Campbell McCutcheon for taking on the project and Amberley Publishing for producing this title.

Otherwise, three blasts on the whistles for the very fine assistance of the senior officers: the late Frank O. Braynard, Tom Cassidy, Richard Faber, Captain James McNamara, William G. Muller (for his superb cover material), Mark Perry (for his evocative foreword) and Don Stoltenberg (for his brilliant artworks).

Junior officers include Robert Allan, Ernest Arroyo, the late Nick Bachko, Dietmar Borchert, Tom Cangialosi, Tom Chirby, the late Frank Cronican, Bill Deibert, the late John Gillespie, Michael Hadgis, Larry A. Hansen, Brad Hatry, Pine Hodges, Charles Howland, Raymond Kane, Robert Lloyd, Vincent Love, Mitchell Mart, Scott McBee, John McFarlane, Abe Michaelson, Fred Rodriguez, the late Captain Robert Russell, Der Scutt, Captain Ed Squire, Dan Trachtenberg, Captain Robin Woodall and Alan Zamchick.

Deep thanks to other crew members: the late Alex Duncan, the late Alvin Grant, Norman Knebel, Rich Romano, Steven L. Tacey and Steffen Weirauch. Companies and other organizations that have assisted include Backer Aerial Photography, Crystal Cruises, Cunard Line, Moran Towing & Transportation Co., Newport News Shipbuilding & Dry Dock Co., Norshipco, Steamship Historical Society of America (especially the Long Island, New York, chapter), South Street Seaport Museum, SS *United States* Conservancy, United States Lines, US Merchant Marine Museum and World Ship Society.

FOREWORD

The SS *United States* has always held a particular fascination for me, perhaps owing to the fact that she so perfectly encapsulates a period in our nation, a history when anything was possible. With her twin rakish funnels and long elegant lines, she suggests power and speed even while at anchor. Her brilliant design by the incomparable William Francis Gibbs proved that nautical form doesn't simply have to follow function, but can flatter it as well. Throughout the 20th Century, maritime supremacy on the North Atlantic was held by the Germans, the French and the English but when the 'Big U' entered service in 1952 and shattered all existing speed records on her maiden voyage, America proved that even though we may have been a tad late to the transatlantic party, we were without question the belle of the ball. Her story is one of American ingenuity, know-how, and triumph. In the years since her premature retirement in 1969, the SS *United States* has suffered more indignities than any other surviving liner, passing from owner to owner, each with their own unrealized plans of bringing her back to service. The latest and most hopeful of these occurred in May 2003 when Norwegian Cruise Line announced their acquisition of our nation's flagship with the stated intention of returning her to active cruise service.

Sadly, by January of 2009, the company abandoned ship and has listed this storied and irreplaceable national treasure for sale. As of this writing, she is still with us, her furnishings and fixtures long auctioned off, her interiors gutted and in ruins. Despite the years of peeling paint and rust, she remains an awe-inspiring sight, pulling against her mooring lines like a thoroughbred race horse anxious to shake free of her reins and set back out to sea. Various preservation groups have united to save her, but time is running out. Her uncertain future, and her unequaled significance in maritime history, prompted me to partner with director Bob Radler in 2008 to produce the award-winning documentary *SS United States: Lady in Waiting* for Chicago and American Public Television. It was our sincere hope that the film would turn a much needed public spotlight onto this largely forgotten symbol of American know-how, and help invigorate efforts by the SS *United States* Conservancy and others to preserve this treasure for future generations as an irreplaceable icon of our nation's proud maritime heritage. Bill Miller's latest book admirably continues this noble mission, and contributes immeasurably to the legacy of the one-and-only 'SS *United States*'.

Mark B. Perry
Los Angeles, California
Producer
SS United States: Lady in Waiting for Chicago's WTTW

INTRODUCTION

When Frank Braynard and I visited the superliner *United States*, then laid up for a full decade at Norfolk, the otherwise busy port along Virginia's Atlantic coast, the ship was in transition. It was June 1979 and the great liner was about to be sold to Seattle-based businessman Richard Hadley for use as a unique condominium-style cruise ship. Although quite dark, very quiet and kept virtually airtight by a de-humidification system, she was still very much the Atlantic ocean liner that we both remembered. The legendary Frank had a far greater and longer association, having been on the delivery trip up from her birthplace at Newport News, very near to Norfolk, and northward for her first arrival at New York, and also made a crossing to Europe. Myself, I could speak and refer only to many visits to the ship, berthed along Manhattan's Luxury Liner Row. On that day, the furniture aboard the *United States*, as an example, was mostly still in place, the crockery stocked in the cupboards and pantries and, except for the stripped, overturned mattresses, the cabins were intact. In ways, it might have been ten days rather than ten years since she had been decommissioned. Passenger notices, such as one for a late afternoon bingo game, were still posted if slightly faded. Copies of the *New York Times* from November 1969 were lying about. Travel brochures along with train and airline schedules were stacked in the excursions office. Thick telephone directories stood on shelves in the telephone office. Vacuum cleaners, some 400 of them, were grouped in order, like soldiers at attention that were awaiting a call to duty. It was all like a stage in one of the Hollywood studios, but after hours, perhaps during the quiet weekend gap. You could almost hear the silence onboard that once busy, people-filled ship. Only the caretakers, a few rather inconspicuous guards, were about. Later, several of Mr Hadley's

representatives – a designer, some planners and the inevitable sales & marketing man – came aboard for a meeting in a specially restored former first-class cabin. It had been freshly painted and carpeted, and looked more late 1970s than early 1950s. Nicholas Bachko, former senior vice president at United States Lines and a man whose knowledge of the ship was probably second only to William Francis Gibbs, the ship's designer, was also aboard that day. He was assisting the small Hadley team.

I peered down the long corridors, into the dining rooms and lounges, and into semi-darkened cabins, and thought back to happier, brighter, certainly busier days. Then there were the mid-day sailings, the festive *bon voyage* parties, spirited deck games and films in the theater, cargo being stowed in the holds and sometimes ferocious Atlantic storms to be faced, on-going maintenance and those annual overhauls down at Newport News, and the legions of passengers, crew and visitors that came and went. I thought also of the small army of celebrities that had sailed the 'Big U' as she was fondly dubbed by so many. There were the luggage-laden Duke and Duchess of Windsor and the Queen of Greece, former Presidents Truman and Eisenhower, Lord Louis Mountbatten and Yugoslavia's Marshal Tito, musical titans such as Irving Berlin and Leonard Bernstein, and of course long lists of Hollywood's golden names: John Wayne and Katharine Hepburn, James Stewart and Mae West, Bob Hope and Rita Hayworth.

The 53,300-ton, 990ft-long *United States*, the third largest liner afloat when she was first commissioned back in 1952, represented the zenith of post-Second World War American design, engineering, mechanics and construction. She was, quite simply, an ocean-going masterpiece. She was the most technologically advanced ocean liner ever built, certainly the fastest and assuredly the safest, and – while not especially notable for her decoration – she was unquestionably one of the cleanest, most spotless, best-maintained ships ever to put to sea.

She was constantly in newspapers and magazines, in newsreels and even feature films, on calendars and candy tins, and was even recreated in toy form and in assemble-yourself miniature models. She was immensely successful, sailing in her years at well over 90 per cent of her capacity, rarely missing a sailing or even being late upon arrival or sailing, and was said to be the most popular single ocean liner of her time. She was the highly coveted Blue Riband champion, the fastest merchant ship afloat. Just about everyone wanted to sail in her or, like myself, at least visit her. In her day, she was said to draw more pre-sailing crowds than any other ship along New York's Luxury Liner Row.

Now, in 2009, as I write this tribute to America's greatest liner (in fact, my third book about the ship), she is, of course, much older, much sadder, in fact a pathetic shell of her once impeccable self. There is much less of her now than during our visit on that warm June day in 1979. Now, she sits silently at a Philadelphia pier – still mentioned in brief sparks, those slightest of rumors, that she might be rebuilt, redecorated and restored as a contemporary cruise ship. But time – and pure economics – have been an enemy. A whole new generation of efficient, purpose-built cruise ships now sail the seas – some as large as 220,000 tons and transporting over 6,000 passengers that are looked after by as many as 1,800 staff and crew. It would hardly be practical, at least from my cushioned-chair perch and otherwise limited calculations, to put her through an expensive and extensive conversion only to compete with the current age of towering, all-white, open-air verandah-lined, lido deck-topped floating resorts. I believe that her future, if there is one at all, is in a non-operational role: a museum ship, even a smartly painted, brilliantly lighted-by-night, moored paperweight, or perhaps – with, say, a rich uncle of sorts in the background – as a floating hotel or convention center. But many actually think, including those devoted and still fascinated by the great SS *United States*, that she will end up at the scrappers, that there is really no alternative purpose for her. They suggest, often in a whispered voice, that her final voyage might be out to the ever-hungry scrappers along the beaches of Alang in distant India.

After this book is completed and then published, I know that there will be more, much more, to be written about the finest American ocean liner of all. But for now, herein is something more of her story: brilliance and triumph, roles in peacetime and potentially in war, a final flourish, great profit and huge popularity, but then the end of an era followed by a long, seemingly endless sleep, times of indecision, decay and even destruction. 2002 marked the 50th anniversary of the record-breaking maiden voyage of the brilliant *United States*. Six years later, on 3 May 2008, in fact my 60th birthday, a glorious one-hour tribute in film entitled *Lady in Waiting: The Story of the SS United States* formally premiered. It was the latest of great tributes to a ship that is still beloved, cherished, even idolized by many. These tributes in both word and film will, I believe, continue. But for now, hopefully this book further marks, commemorates and documents, even in small ways, the life and times of this greatest and grandest of ships.

Bill Miller
Secaucus
New Jersey
December 2008

An intimate, cheerful cocktail bar highlights the Cabin Smoking Room. In this room good fellowship is inspired by the congenial atmosphere and the pleasant decorations. (J&C McCutcheon Collection)

The Cabin Dining Saloon is midnight blue ... the curtains are a combination of green and red stripes. Here, with quiet indirect lighting, brilliant scupltures in bas-relief, gleaming china and silver and snowy white table linen, is the perfect setting for mealtime at sea. (J&C McCutcheon Collection)

The Tourist Smoking Room is located on the Main Deck and extends the full width of the ship. The pleasant, well-stocked bar is done in decorative glass ... and there is a bar service until the early hours of the morning. (J&C McCutcheon Collection)

Aluminum motifs by Erica Egan show eighteenth and nineteenth century sailors and sea life inn the Tourist Dining Saloon. (J&C McCutcheon Collection)

Chapter I

TEST RUN: THE BEAUTIFUL *AMERICA*

Many ocean liner historians and enthusiasts rate the *America* as one of the most beautiful, if not the most beautiful passenger ship, ever to sail under the flag of the United States. She was a ship of extreme good looks – twin masts and twin funnels on a well-balanced, black hull against a snow-white superstructure. She was an improvement of the Grace Line's albeit smaller *Santa Rosa* quartet of 1932-33 (*Santa Rosa*, *Santa Paula*, *Santa Elena* and *Santa Lucia*) and then the prototype of the much larger *United States* of 1952. But to others, it was the *America*'s interiors that made her most special. They were not only very luxurious, but quite handsome. They were also intimate, charming, cozily inviting. Many United States Lines loyalists actually preferred sailing onboard the *America* over the far larger and certainly far faster *United States*. Some liked the added sea time that the *America* provided – six days from New York to Southampton and Le Havre, for example, as compared to the five days of the *United States*. In the 1950s, the *America* belonged to a class of Atlantic liners that included the likes of Holland America's *Nieuw Amsterdam*, American Export's *Independence* and *Constitution*, the Italian Line's *Andrea Doria* and *Cristoforo Colombo*, French Line's *Ile de France* and Cunard's *Mauretania*, *Caronia* and *Britannic*. They were medium-sized luxury liners.

'Until the advent of the *United States* in the early 1950s, the United States Lines was never quite in the same league on the prestigious, very competitive North Atlantic run as, say, Cunard, White Star, the French Line and the two Germans, the Hamburg America Line and North German Lloyd', reflected Richard Faber, a New York-based ocean liner collectibles dealer.

Neither was the United States Lines senior to those companies, but instead was created just after the First World War, in 1920, when there was a shortage of European passenger ships. The company opened for business that summer, using US Government-owned, mostly former German passenger ships. The 9,900grt *Susquehana* was, in fact, their very first ship and sailed from New York to Bremerhaven and then on to Danzig. Numerous other ships followed, highlighted by the 59,956grt *Leviathan*, the former *Vaterland* of Hamburg America, which joined in 1923. America's first superliner, she was in fact a misfit, barely earned her way and was not replaced after being prematurely retired in 1934 (and then sent to the scrappers four years later). Otherwise, through various changes, owners and the upheaval of the worldwide Depression of the 1930s, the company generally maintained a moderate, quite conservative approach, creating new tonnage such as the 24,200-ton sisters *Manhattan* and *Washington* in 1932-33 and then the 33,900grt *America* in 1940. They were the largest newly-built American liners to date. Thoughts of a larger ship, in fact an American-built superliner, were stirred largely by the Second World War and, in great part, by possible future need for large troop transports. The *America* was the progressive follow-up, with improvements and slightly greater size, to the *Manhattan* and *Washington*. At 33,900 tons, she was larger by 10,000 tons than those 24,200grt sisters; she was also longer, at 723ft, compared to the 705ft of the earlier pair. Their passenger quarters were quite similar, however: 580 in cabin class, 461 tourist class and 196 third class on the *Manhattan*, for example, and 515 first, 371 cabin and 159 tourist on the *America*.

All three had steam-turbine propulsion and, while designed to be weekly transatlantic running-mates if the war had not intervened by 1940, at the time of the *America*'s completion, the new ship was actually faster by 2 knots, with a service speed of 23 knots. The first two ships came from the New York Shipbuilding Corporation, Camden, New Jersey, while the *America*, like the *Santa Rosa* and her three sisters, was launched from the mighty Newport News Shipbuilding & Dry Dock Company at Newport News in Virginia. Coincidentally, all three suffered from the same problem in their earliest days: their funnels proved to be too short, sending smoke onto the aft decks. On each ship, the stacks were soon heightened and, from general consensus, this actually seemed to improve their overall appearance. Clearly, the *America* was the great prototype to the *United States*. 'She was the version', noted ocean liner enthusiast Alan Zamchick, 'that William Francis Gibbs was improving the art of ship design and construction.' The *America* was a great ship leading to a greater ship. But she was a special, highly beloved liner in her own right. She had the qualities of a pre-war liner, in class with the likes of the *Niuew Amsterdam* (completed in 1938) and the second *Mauretania* (1939).

She was not an express liner, however, and not simply the big hotel that sped across the seas. Instead, she was cozy and had a great warmth about her. Actually, the *America* was almost European in style.

Laid down on 22 August 1938, the twin-screw *America* was actually the first ship in the US Maritime Commission's program to rebuild, enlarge and strengthen the American merchant marine. Over 6,000 passenger ships, freighters, tankers and other craft followed. The *America* was Building Order Number One. With the project completed, by 1952, the *United States* was the last. Eleanor Roosevelt, the wife of President Franklin D. Roosevelt, looked after the naming of the ship at the launching on 31 August 1939. A day later, most dramatically, the Nazis invaded Poland and, within days, the Second World War had started. In the following months, as the liner was completed and then fitted out, her intended service between New York and Northern Europe seemed less and less likely. Even the *Manhattan* and *Washington* were soon switched over to evacuation sailings, routed in and out of the Mediterranean and western Europe rather than the traditional Channel ports and, quite obviously, Nazi Germany. Cruises, specially created for American tourists still able to ignore the dramatically serious events in Europe, were organized by the United States Lines as a commercial, revenue-making alternative. These one-class, leisure voyages took the *Manhattan*, *Washington* and *America*, (beginning with her maiden voyage in August 1940) to Bermuda, the Bahamas, the Caribbean and through the Panama Canal on inter-coastal itineraries to Los Angeles and San Francisco in California. It was all rather short-lived however.

By the summer of 1941, some six months before the United States officially entered the war following the attack by the Japanese on Pearl Harbor, the year-old *America* was taken over by the US Navy, refitted as a high-capacity troopship (with an official wartime capacity listed as 8,175) and, for security reasons, renamed USS *West Point*. Her urgent, top-secret voyages took the all-gray-painted ex-liner to ports around the globe.

A sampling of her Wartime career might begin in January 1942 when she departed the US East Coast to deliver troops to India and then to Australia and New Zealand. She continued around the world by finishing that voyage at San Francisco. She then returned to Australia before traveling to New York, in July 1942, via the Panama Canal. Next, she made two hurried voyages across the North Atlantic to British ports and then steamed from New York to distant Bombay via Rio de Janeiro and the South African Cape. From India, she sailed homeward via the Pacific to San Francisco and followed with a trip to Australia, New Zealand and remote Noumea. In February 1943, she departed from San Francisco on an around-the-world voyage taking in Australia, India, Port Suez, Massawa, Aden, Capetown, Rio de Janeiro and finally New York. This was followed by two round trips between New York and Casablanca, and then another trip to Bombay via Rio and Capetown. She eventually reached San Francisco and made three trips to Honolulu. By early 1944, she was making regular trips to the South Pacific, including calls at Sydney, and then, that summer, headed for Boston for a string of crossings to ports in the UK.

In 1945, she made many more voyages, from New York and Hampton Roads (near Norfolk) as well as Boston to French and Italian ports in the western Mediterranean, often via Oran and Gibraltar. Her last Navy trip was, in fact, her longest to date: leaving Boston in December 1945 via the Panama Canal for Pearl Harbor and then Manila before re-crossing the Pacific to Panama and then arriving in New York, where she docked in February 1946. She did have several close calls during the war, but managed to escape unharmed and accident-free.

In February 1946, at New York, the USS *West Point* was renamed *America* and returned to the United States Lines; her valiant, heroic war duties were complete. Quickly, she was dispatched to Newport News, to her builder's yard, where her reconditioning for luxury, peacetime service began. Completely outfitted to the highest commercial standards, she entered North Atlantic liner service – between New York, Le Havre and Southampton – in November 1946. Briefly, for several months before, the United States Lines made do with an interim service, using a chartered troopship, Moore McCormack Lines' 20,600grt *Argentina*. Among her passengers were the Duke and Duchess of Windsor, who returned to their home in Paris following a long wartime exile in the Bahamas. They crossed from New York aboard the *Argentina* in the summer of 1945.

During the War, the *Manhattan* and *Washington* had been very useful military troop transports, sailing as the USS *Wakefield* and USS *Mount*

Vernon respectively. But while the *Wakefield* (ex-*Manhattan*) was thoroughly repaired and rebuilt following a very serious fire at sea in September 1942, she was declared surplus soon after the War ended, in 1946, and sent to the US Government's reserve ship fleet along the upper Hudson River, at Stony Point, New York. The former *Washington* was partially restored, with 1,106 all tourist-class berths and under her original name, for United States Lines austerity service until October 1951, running voyages between New York, Southampton, Le Havre and Bremerhaven. Afterward, she was managed by the newly formed Military Sea Transportation Service, which looked after Government passengers and troops, but on civilian-manned and operated vessels. Again, she was used on the North Atlantic. She was, however, finally retired and sent, in February 1953, to the mothball fleet on the upper Hudson River. She was moored alongside her onetime sister, the former *Manhattan*, and the USS *Edmund B. Alexander* (the former *America* of 1905) and about 200 other ships that were being held for a possible national emergency. Most of them, however, would never again see a day's service.

Earlier, in the summer of 1952, it was rumored that the San Francisco-based American President Lines would lease the *Washington* from the Federal Government for use as a low-fare, austerity-style transpacific liner. According to initial planning, she would join the luxury liners *President Cleveland* and *President Wilson*, but not on the same general, luxury standard. The *Washington* would have replaced two transports with some austere passenger quarters, the *General W.H. Gordon* and *General M.C. Meigs*, used recently in Pacific service. Nothing ever came of this proposal for the twenty-year-old ship, however. Long past their useful lives and while looked over by foreign buyers for possible upgrades and conversions to commercial liners, both former United States Lines passenger ships were cleared finally by the US Government for scrapping in the early 1960s. The ex-*Manhattan* was towed to a Kearny, New Jersey, shipbreaker's yard in July 1964 and *Washington* followed in June 1965.

After President Truman signed into law the Displaced Persons Program in December 1945, the first group of 800, most of them released from the Nazi concentration camps, sailed from Bremerhaven for New York aboard a 12,000-ton troopship, the United States Lines-chartered *Marine Flasher*, in May 1946. Two days later, a sister ship, the *Marine Perch*, followed from that otherwise still war-ravaged port. During the next three years, these ships together with six others – *Marine Marlin*, *Marine Falcon*, *Marine Jumper*, *Marine Tiger*, *Marine Shark* and the specially named *Ernie Pyle* – were chartered in conjunction with the US State Department and the US Bureau of Immigration to carry occupation forces, their dependents, war brides, returning prisoners of war and displaced person alongside businessmen, students, even

The 24,000-ton sisters *Manhattan* (1932), seen here departing from New York, and *Washington* (1933) were in ways prototypes to the *United States*, commissioned twenty years later. (Alex Duncan)

the first waves of European-bound economy tourists. These ships were by no means luxury vessels, but adequate, 'clean and well-fed' passenger-carrying ships that served a much-needed purpose in those otherwise hard-pressed, passenger-ship short times. They made scheduled voyages from New York to Southampton and Le Havre, but also to Antwerp, Bremerhaven and even up to Scandinavian and Baltic ports such as Oslo, Copenhagen and Gdynia. But then, with the great bulk of their work completed by the fall of 1949, they were phased out and returned to their US Government owners, mostly then to be mothballed as part of the Federal Reserve Fleet in the James River in Virginia. They were cleared for sale to commercial owners in the early 1960s and were subsequently rebuilt as freighters, bulk carriers, even early-generation container ships. While a few were later lost to accidents (the former *Marine Perch* was, for example, sunk off Gibraltar in June 1978), the others were eventually retired and finished up at the breakers.

So, by the late 1940s, as the United States Lines was busily constructing its new super ship, the *America* maintained singlehandedly transatlantic service, assisted by the austere, low-fare, partially restored *Washington* and the eight transports mentioned above. Expectedly, the *America* was immensely popular from the start of her post-War revival.

The *America* was a luxury ship and was like a brand-new liner as she set off on her post-war maiden voyage in November 1946, according to Raymond

Kane, a member of her newly installed United States Lines crew. 'I joined the National Maritime Union in 1946. It was just after the war and they were tough times in many ways. Jobs in particular were in short supply. So, a job with the Union and especially aboard a virtually new liner was, as we called it, a feeding and sleeping job. I was assigned to the *America* and sent down by train from New York to the Newport News Shipyard to help prepare her. She was the first American luxury liner to enter service following the War. But few American crewmembers had experience with luxury liners. We were mostly a nation of merchant seamen, the crews of freighters and tankers and transports, but not first-rate luxury ships. We sailed up to New York aboard her. She was in beautiful condition. She sparkled.'

Kane spent the next years aboard the largest, fastest and finest liner in the US fleet. 'We sailed regularly between New York, Le Havre and Southampton in those days', he recalled.

'There was a turn-around in New York of three or four days and usually an overnight at Southampton on the other end. I began as an elevator operator and then went to bellboy. All the bellboys then wore pillbox hats and, in winter, also a cape for gangway watch. We would welcome passengers at the gangways, at Pier 61 in New York and, at Southampton and Le Havre, from the boat trains arriving from London and Paris. I later went to cabin class and then to first class. Elevator boys, while a lower rank, actually did better, sometimes making $100 extra each at the end of a voyage, and actually made more money than, say, a New York City policeman in the late 1940s. A bell captain was the very best job, however. You opened the dining room doors and so knew everyone. You were alert to the best people, the most prominent names, the most important United States Lines passengers and home office personnel. You offered them a collection of the voyage menus and then graciously bade them farewell. You were often given $2 per passenger in first class and so 500 passengers meant $1,000. This was divided between the bell captain and the assistant bell captain, and amounted to $500 each per trip. That was big money back then. And it was a virtual monopoly for the bell captain and the assistant bell captain. Of course, it was all shipboard politics. You even helped select the best tables in the dining room. We had lots of celebrities on the *America* in the late '40s. There was virtually no air competition at that time. We had members of the great American families, the Rockefellers and the Phipps's, and also Margaret Truman and, of course, all the theatrical and Hollywood types. I remember Red Skelton spent his evenings drinking and telling stories to the bell boys. The *America* was the peak of travel for prominent people on the European run,' he added.

'She was an absolutely beautiful ship. The first-class ballroom was superb with engraved glass panels. For added service, we had English stewards in the smoking room, who were specially naturalized to serve on an American vessel. She was immaculate from stem to stern. Every day at sea, the staff captain, the first assistant engineer and the yeoman did a white glove inspection everywhere onboard. God forbid there was any dirt or dust! The *America* was a grand shuttle to and from Europe in those days. The late Captain Robert Russell was a young cadet aboard the *America* in the summer of 1957 and made two transatlantic round voyages aboard her. 'She was the biggest ship I had ever been aboard at that time.'

'She was well organized, very neat, an immaculately clean ship. She was also a good steering ship. Captain Fender was then her master and he later sent a congratulatory letter to me. I took the wheel two hours a day and also did lots of radar navigation. I also helped with the caring for the lifeboats by draining them. As a cadet, you were given first-class menus at meals and wore dress blues at dinner. For a young man, being aboard the *America* was a great experience.'

Vincent Love joined United States Lines' New York offices in 1959 and initially was assigned to the Pre-Paid Passenger Department. 'We carried lots of German immigrants on the westbound crossings in the 1950s and into the '60s. These passengers had their passages paid for them by German relatives already in the US. I made the reservations and, of course, these were mostly in tourist class. I also had to greet the immigrants, arriving on the *America* and *United States*, at Pier 86. There were lots of them and it was big business for United States Lines then.'

Love well recalled the *America*. 'She was the smaller of our two liners, of course, and so we dubbed her the baby *United States*. In fact, she was more comfortable, had Art Deco touches, but was not as overly luxurious when compared to many European liners. Also, quite sadly, she was not a happy ship, especially in her later years. One of her captains was said to be unpopular and this filtered down through the ranks and then too she had lots of labor problems. There were frequent disputes, even racial conflicts among her crew. And, of course, she also did not have much reserve speed and so could fall off schedule if delayed. In contrast, the *United States* had great reserve speed and so was rarely late.'

Today, the United States Lines' archives are housed just outside New York City, at the US Merchant Marine Museum at Kings Point, New York. Daniel Trachtenberg, who also served with the SS *United States* Foundation, was both an assistant and an archivist at the museum. He helped organize masses of material brought over from 1 Broadway, the company's Lower Manhattan headquarters, which were closed down in the spring of 1979.

'Among the items at Kings Point, there are many folders, envelopes and even blueprints labeled *America* Replacement', he reported. 'The Company always planned to use two liners and so there was a new companion being considered for the *United States*. After 1952, a new liner was projected to cost a very costly $100 million, which then went up to $110 million. She was to be a smaller ship, planned at about 40,000 tons, but was to have a high speed, over 30 knots. But there was less and less interest in the late 1950s on the part of the Eisenhower administration in Washington, especially in the face of airline competition and therefore declining passenger ship loads, no matter how slight at first. And so, the United States Lines decided to keep the *America*. As she began carrying fewer and fewer passengers, the company remained optimistic and often stated "we hope to make up losses next year".'

By the early 1960s, the *America* began to slip further and further, carrying fewer passengers, showing greater losses and all the while aging as well. Resourcefully, the United States Lines sent her on more popular off-season cruises to the likes of Bermuda, Nassau and San Juan. But it was merely a temporary measure, 'a Band-Aid for the widening hole that was the increasingly costly American passenger ship fleet', said one former officer. A big blow came in September 1963, just hours before she was to sail from Pier 86 on another Atlantic crossing. A flash strike erupted on board following a dispute among some crew members over the use of toilet facilities. The entire incident, embarrassing and disruptive as it was, had racial undertones. No adequate, quick solution could be reached and so the sailing was canceled, the passengers sent back ashore and the ship laid up. She was soon taken over to the Todd Shipyard in Hoboken, New Jersey, little more than a mile from her Manhattan berth, and, with months of sailings canceled, sat out much of the winter as a dark, lonely, all but empty ship.

Rumors circulated that she would be retired completely, but in fact she did resume sailing in February. It was her final season with United States Lines. The following November she was sold, for $1.5 million, to the Greek-flag Chandris Lines, to a subsidiary of theirs called Okeania S.A. She would be among the first American liners to be sold foreign and so hoist new colors. Rebuilt at Piraeus in the Chandris shipyard, which was little more than an anchorage using work boats and floating warehouses, her capacity was more than doubled, from 1,046 to 2,258, now all-tourist class. She was renamed *Australis* (meaning 'Australian Maiden') and ranked as the largest liner in the otherwise very large Greek merchant marine. She was placed on the booming Europe-Australia and low-fare around-the-world services. Her itineraries often varied slightly, but generally were routed as a three-month trip: Bremerhaven, Rotterdam, Southampton, Gibraltar, Naples, Malta, Piraeus, Port Said, Aden, Fremantle, Melbourne, Sydney, Auckland, Papeete, Acapulco, Balboa, Cristobal, Port Everglades and return to Southampton. She joined the 1,642-passenger *Ellinis*, another former American, the onetime Matson Line's *Lurline*, and was later assisted by the likes of the *Queen Frederica*, which had been the Gibbs-designed *Malolo* (and later *Matsonia*), and then the *Britanis*, also from Matson, having been the *Monterey*, then the *Matsonia* and a subsequent *Lurline*.

The all-white *Australis* once returned to New York for a twelve-hour call in April 1970. She berthed at Pier 84, just across from her once regular United States Lines slip at Pier 86. She was accorded a small tugboat reception upon arrival and was dressed overall in flags by day, strands of lights by night. Brad Hatry, a keen passenger ship observer and onetime chairman of the World Ship Society's Port of New York Branch, was among the visitors to the former *America*.

'She was completely full, over 2,000 passengers, on an around-the-world voyage', he remembered. 'Passengers had paid as little as $1,200 for an inside double down on a lower deck but for the entire eighty-day trip. I especially recall that there were three sittings of forty-five minutes each in the dining rooms: early, main and late.' But as the Australian and around-the-world trades fell away, mostly due to aircraft competition, for Chandris in the 1970s the future of the aging *Australis* grew more and more uncertain. Dimitri Kaparis, the chief naval architect at Chandris, had made a proposal to Anthony Chandris, the ship's owner. 'I worked out a plan how, for $18 million, we could convert the *Australis* from steam to more efficient diesel', recounted Kaparis. 'I further planned that we use her on three- and four-day cruises out of Miami, which I felt had great potential. Unfortunately, Mr Chandris was against the idea. He felt that $18 million was too much money when put against the ship's then thirty-eight years of age. Instead, we put the *Australis* up for sale (fall 1977).'

She returned to New York in the spring of 1978, but then, with less than adequate repairs and upgrading, she was pressed into cruise service as the renamed *America*. Her new owners, Venture Cruise Lines (also called America Cruise Lines), could not have been more inexperienced or less prepared. On her first short cruise, on 30 June, there were reports of insufficient food, poor service, poor safety conditions and, worst of all, garbage being stored in the swimming pool and sightings of rats. Such indignity for the former flagship of the entire American merchant marine! She was soon arrested for debt, on 8 July, and seized by US Government marshals and then laid up at Pier 92, at the foot of West 52 Street in Manhattan.

Bob Allan, an ocean liner historian and architect, saw the *America* in her final months, in that scandal-ridden summer of 1978. 'I had seen the *United States* and so immediately began to make a comparison,' he explained. 'The *America*, even in her demoded, almost miserable state under the short-lived

The *America*, but seen here in Lower New York Bay during the Second World War as the troopship USS *West Point*. (Ernest Arroyo Collection)

Venture Cruise Lines, was lighter and more cheerful in decoration than the *United States*. The older ship was warmer, cozier, with glamorous 1940s spaces. Perhaps she was even the very best of 1940s liners. She had some wonderful features: that gallery above the lounge, brass handrails, magnificent elevator casings. I recall that the chairs in the lounge had beautiful floral prints on them, bright red roses on the seat and back cushions. She also had great scale. She was not too big. Onboard the much larger *United States* by comparison, it was always a time-consuming matter to get around.'

But sadly, the revived *America* was in absolutely miserable condition. Having been sold that spring by Chandris to Venture for $5 million, the faded ship was auctioned off that August for only $1 million and, surprisingly, went back to Chandris again. She was brought to Greece, given some repairs, lost her forward funnel in the process and then re-emerged in April 1979 as the *Italis*. She ran only in the Mediterranean, however, but then was laid up permanently that fall. Like the *United States* after her lay-up in 1969, the ex-*America* hereafter faced an uncertain future, one often spiced with rumors,

tales, even the very occasional accuracy. By October 1980, for example, it was widely reported that she was going to Ghana in West Africa to become a Swiss-operated hotel ship. She was even renamed *Noga* in preparation. The so-called Noga Corporation was said to be the ship's new owners, but nothing came to pass and, by 1984, she had passed to Silver Moon Ferries Ltd, who renamed her *Alferdoss*. But as she continued to rust at her moorings in Eleusis Bay, near Piraeus, the rumors continued: use as a floating prison at Galveston in Texas, an exhibition center in Montreal, a trade fair ship at Shanghai, a yacht club in Australia and a hotel moored along the Manhattan waterfront as the Hotel America. Scrap merchants were often mentioned as well. In the summer of 1992, when the equally faded, mystery-shrouded *United States* had reached Turkey and with the former *America* in nearby Greece, the two, once proud fleet mates were closer in location than they had been for years.

The long-neglected older ship was sold in 1992, in fact, to interests in far-off Thailand, who planned to make her an ocean-liner-style hotel near Bangkok. She was renamed *American Star* and prepared for the long, slow tow out to the East via the South African Cape (Suez Canal authorities refused the aged, weakened ship the right to pass through the canal in fear she might take on water and even sink). In fact, her days were numbered, but she was lost instead, in the eastern Atlantic. After passing through the Straits of Gibraltar, she was lashed by a ferocious storm, the towlines snapped and the ship was sent crashing onto a rocky beach in the otherwise remote north end of the Canary Islands. The four caretaker crewmen who were aboard were rescued by helicopter. She was abandoned as a wreck and in time, with continuous strong seas and high winds, her midsection gave way and the 723ft-long ship broke in two. The aft 300ft section soon became canted and so created a even more pathetic sight. She was a complete ruin. In time, that section released itself, drifted out to sea and then sank. The remaining 400ft of the ship has been stripped by local fishermen, some of whom perished in their efforts. By 2000, the Spanish navy was thinking of destroying the wreckage with explosives. Then, in 2007, that forward section toppled, fell into the sea and sank. It was indeed a very sad end to that once very great ship.

Left: Seen here on 2 October 1946, the *America* is being reconditioned for return to peacetime luxury service. A supervisor at the Newport News Shipyard stands atop the large hammerhead crane and which overlooks another liner being transformed, the *Santa Rosa* of the Grace Line. Both ships were designs of William Francis Gibbs. (Frank O. Braynard Collection)

Right: The revived *Washington* as seen in 1948, but used only in austerity service on the North Atlantic. (Gillespie-Faber Collection)

Above left: A New York dockside view of the *America*. (Author's Collection)

Above right: The *America* docking at Bremerhaven. (Richard Faber Collection)

Left: The beautiful *America* at Pier 86. (Author's Collection)

Right: Chandris colors, the *Australis* (ex-*America*) at New York for the first time since October 1964. The date of photo is 21 April 1970. (Author's Collection)

Below left: Restored as the cruise ship *America* for the shortlived Venture Cruise Lines, the liner is seen here in 1978. (Author's Collection)

Below right: Sad ending: the remains of the former *America* after breaking in two in the north end of the Canary Islands. This photo dates from 2005. (Steven L. Tacey)

Left: After the Second World War and through the 1950s, the United States Lines maintained up to fifty-five cargo vessels such as the 7,600-ton *American Chief,* which carried twelve passengers on transatlantic crossings. (United States Lines)

Right: New, larger and faster cargo vessels came on the line in the 1960s, ships such as the 11,000-ton *American Commander* of 1963. With her raked, tapered funnel, she had a definite link to the *United States.* (Alex Duncan).

Chapter II

CREATING THE BIG SHIP

The *United States* was in many ways the most unique ship of all time. She was the very finest vessel in the American merchant marine, the country's greatest ocean liner and one of the most important ships, passenger or otherwise, of the twentieth century. 'The *United States* was a pacesetter', noted Mitchell Mart, an ocean liner historian and well-known seller of passenger ship memorabilia. 'She had innovations galore. She was known everywhere in America, probably everywhere in the world. She had a profile that was as strong as the USA itself and as distinctive as the Empire State Building. Nearly sixty years later, she is very strong in the ocean liner collectible market place. For my business, she is one of the top dozen super star sellers, in a class with the Cunard Queens, CGT's *France* and the big Italians.'

New York-based architect and world-class ship model collector Der Scutt added, 'the *United States* stood alone and apart from many other liners designed and built in the 1940s and 1950s. Alone, her exterior profile was magnificently proportioned, probably more pleasing than any other ocean liner afloat. Her image was memorable and symbolized sleekness with unrivaled authority. Her majestic stacks, for example, epitomized skyscraper giganticism. Her hull was designed for unsurpassed speed, obviously to outrace U-boats and other enemy warships, should the call come to go to war. From top to bottom, her bow appears as an incredible knife. Some bows push away the water; the *United States*'s cut the water! The slender profile promised a kind of modernity with a convincing ocean-going superiority. The big Cunard Queens both had big girths; the slim shape and rounded stern of the *United States* was the gentle finale to the graceful efficiency of the hull. The *United States* slopes down to the waterline in an elegant contoured curve whereas the sterns of the *Queen Mary*

and *Queen Elizabeth* are rounded and sort of plopped into the water. Bubbling water followed the Queens' sterns; crashing turbulence made up the wake of the American flagship with unprecedented intensity. The *United States* will always be remembered for her ocean presence, which embodied dignity, proficiency, speed and service. There has never been a similar likeness of image and icon.

Tom Chirby, a passenger ship enthusiast with a great interest in maritime preservation, appreciates the *United States* and hopes that she will be saved, preferably as a museum. 'She must be preserved and saved as a great piece of American history. She was the pinnacle of American marine engineering, the apex of technology. With the *United States*, America proved its mechanical superiority. She was the ultimate ocean liner, the ultimate merchant ship. Just about everything about her was unique. Even her construction was unique – she was floated out from her building berth rather than launched traditionally, for example, and that was very different back in 1951. She was the peak. There was no better ship!'

The creation of the *United States* was every bit a national project. While she was actually constructed at Newport News, Virginia, just about every state provided something. The blueprint paper, for example, was rooted in the woodlands of Maine and was brought to New York City by freight train and then by barge. In all, 145,000 pounds of paper, the equivalent of two freight cars, was used by the Gibbs & Cox offices in Lower Manhattan for the *United States* project. These blueprints were then shipped in cartons made in North Carolina to Newport News and then to Washington for final approval. There were metals used aboard the ship were from Idaho and Montana, clocks from Connecticut, tools from Rhode Island, radar equipment from Massachusetts and the likes of gears and pumps from Wisconsin. Safety, of course, dominated the design and construction processes of the liner. Her resistance to collision, for example, was twice that required by international standards. Her subdivided hull was easily equal to that of a warship. While hundreds of thousands of slabs of lumber were used during the construction, the only wood allowed aboard after completion, it was often said, was in the butcher's blocks and several pianos. The fireproofing of the ship was to the extreme. Even curtains and furniture coverings were flame-proofed and all interior paints were fire retardant. No less than seven Government agencies oversaw her construction: the American Bureau of Shipping, the US Navy, the Maritime Administration, US Public Health, the Federal Communications Commission, US Customs Service and the US Coast Guard. She was noteworthy in many ways. She had, for example, the largest funnels afloat. She had more aluminum in her construction than any other ship: hand rails, lifeboats, those stacks and even large sections of the superstructure. She was the first American passenger ship to be built in a dry dock, the first to exacting US Navy rather than commercial standards and the first US-flag Atlantic passenger ship to be so named since 1847.

But the propulsion machinery for the *United States* was perhaps of the greatest interest. She was intended from the start to be the fastest liner yet built, having capability of the greatest speed ever seen for a commercial vessel and indeed producing the highest record for crossings on the Atlantic. 'When she was finally completed in 1952, it was thought that the *United States* used her maximum power, especially for her record-breaking maiden voyages, both east and westbound', commented Captain Ed Squire, who sailed the ship on several short voyages and later commanded such vessels as the Staten Island ferryboats in New York harbor. 'Actually, her power plant was a closely guarded secret, by Mr Gibbs as well as by the US Government (in particular the US Navy), because of her intended dual purpose as a commercial liner and wartime troop carrier. In fact, she was designed as the greatest naval auxiliary of her time. But it was not until she was declassified by tight naval security in 1968, sixteen years after her maiden voyage, that it was revealed that she never ran at full power capacity. Only six of her eight boilers were used during her voyages. The boilers were, in fact, rotated for maintenance purposes and the six operating boilers were run at an average of 60 per cent. Even during the maiden voyage, the main engines were not opened up all the way. The Navy did not want her to be run at a speed of 40 knots or more. She had eight specially built Babcox & Wilcox boilers in two separate fire rooms. Ten oil burners on the front of each boiler gives one an idea of the enormous capacity of these boilers. It was believed that the total capacity of these boilers was more than the turbines could take. This was quite remarkable for the early 1950s and for a merchant ship. Her power plant was, in fact, the same as that

used on the USS *Midway*, a US Navy class of aircraft carriers, begun in 1943 and later used aboard the super-carrier *Forrestal* of 1954. Furthermore, while the shape of her hull, which was kept under tight security until 1968, was actually much like other big Atlantic liners, she had two, five-bladed inboard propellers for greater speed. Without question, she was a wonder of her time, indeed, a very great, magnificent ship!'

The preliminary blueprints and drawings from 1946 of what would become the *United States* are in the United States Lines archives at the US Merchant Marine Museum at Kings Point. According to Daniel Trachtenberg, a one-time museum curator, Gibbs actually made his first serious drawings in 1943, but began projecting for the superliner as early as 1940, twelve years before she would enter service. By 1946, the project was technically known as Maritime Administration P-6 Troopship. It was often said at Gibbs & Cox that William Francis Gibbs actually designed many variations of the *United States* from quick sketches to preliminary architectural renderings. He hoped to see other versions built, some slightly smaller. One plan became the 43,000grt *President Washington*, a proposed transpacific superliner for American President Lines for 1957. But after the mid-1950s, Washington became less and less interested in passenger ships, especially large ones, and without the Government's financial help there could be no new American liners. Even their alternative value as troop transports in time of emergency seemed to diminish as a factor. Gibbs did see two smaller versions of the *United States* actually come about: Grace Line's 300-passenger sisters *Santa Rosa* and *Santa Paula* of 1958. Almost everything about their exterior design was based on the larger ship with the obvious exception that they had a single funnel.

Gibbs was an extraordinary man. Born in 1886, he was a graduate of Harvard University and held a law degree from Columbia University. He hated the law, however, and taught himself naval architecture. Earlier, he and his brother Frederic used to make ship designs spread out on the floor of their family home in Philadelphia. Just for fun on Saturday afternoons, they used to redesign existing British battleships. In time, William Francis was especially known for his brilliant concepts in ship design and planning shipboard details while Frederic was seen as the financial and administrative genius. William Francis especially liked ocean liners, however, and presented the Government during the First World War with formal plans for his proposed superliner service that included a shipping terminal at the eastern end of Long Island, at Montauk Point, so as to save trans-ocean passage times. Together, the brothers formed their own company in 1922 and seven years later merged with Daniel H. Cox, a celebrated yacht and small craft designer, and formed Gibbs & Cox. William Francis built a great list of credits: he had redesigned the *Leviathan* (1921-23), created the safety-advanced *Malolo* (1927) and produced the *Santa*

Rosa quartet (1932). In all, some 6,000 naval and commercial ships were built to Gibbs & Cox specifications, many of them coming from the company's 21 West Street offices, in Lower Manhattan, which at its peak employed over 3,000. Fourteen of the fifteen floors were under tight security to protect models, plans and top-secret Navy projects. A simple, ascetic man in ways, he was also a tough taskmaster and himself worked seven days a week. It was not uncommon to find him at his office early on a Sunday morning.

'I was often called at home, even at one in the morning, by William Francis', recalled a onetime top assistant. 'He went straight into business. There were no excuses. Once, he woke me well after midnight just to say that he had decided to reduce the height of the radar mast on the *United States* by two feet!' However, Gibbs somehow found time for his other interests: opera, theater, books, baseball and firefighting. He even designed the *Firefighter* (1935), the greatest fireboat yet built, for the City of New York and often proudly told friends, 'she can throw water seventy-four floors up the Empire State Building.' Gibbs also made the basic plan for the 2,000 Liberty ships built during the Second World War, other freighters as well as battleships and heavy cruisers. He saw the *America* as a beginning to his lifelong goal: to create the world's greatest ocean liner and sail her under the US flag. He was fiercely patriotic and, while respectful, he actually resented ships such as the *Queen Mary* and the *Normandie*. 'He often lost his temper, but one of the worst occasions was when he discovered two French engineers unofficially looking around the engine rooms onboard the *United States*', according to a former crewmember.

'Just as many young boys were taken to baseball games, I was once told that in boyhood, William Francis Gibbs was taken to watch fires', recalled Bill Deibert, a naval architect. 'He became fascinated by fire – its causes, how it evolved and how it was extinguished.' This fascination appeared in increasing force in the design of his ships and especially with the design of *United States*. He had also been deeply influenced and affected by the tragic loss of another superliner, *Normandie*, at her New York City pier in 1942, at the height of the Second World War. Gibbs was firm that this could never happen to his superliner even when she was nothing more than highly secret files of ideas, projections and preliminary sketches. Furthermore, the US Navy, then in charge of the *Normandie*, had not forgotten her demise. Fire could be deadly to ships, especially to big ocean liners. Gibbs was dedicated to the *United States* beyond any of his other creations. He called ship-to-shore every day and spoke with William Kaiser, the Chief Engineer, and discussed as well as questioned every aspect of the liner's operation and performance. On arrival, after a quick breakfast in his Fifth Avenue apartment, he hurried down to the Brooklyn shoreline in his chauffeur-driven Cadillac and watched the inbound *United States*. Foul weather never stopped him. Afterward, the car raced to Pier 86, where he was one of the first to board and, a staff member later recalled, 'he stalked through the ship, almost deck by deck, and checked instruments and records.' He was often the scourge of a shipbuilder, however. An old friend, formerly with the Newport News Shipyard, added, 'he was not especially liked by many. He moved into the Yard, set up an office and practically haunted the place, tapping around at all hours, testing materials and reordering equipment that did not meet his high specifications.

In later years, Gibbs often watched from his Lower Manhattan office window as the *United States* sailed past, outbound for Europe. He died on 6 September 1967 and, on her next outbound sailing, as the liner reached the lower Hudson, she slowed and gave a thunderous whistle salute to America's finest twentieth-century marine architect and engineer. In creating the *United States*, Gibbs realized early on that the US Government would probably pay for half of the ship's construction, considering her alternative use as a troopship in case of war. But he went further and convinced officials in Washington that the liner required extra defense features such as extra speed and twin engine rooms. As usual, he was successful and obtained the extra funding. Actually, Gibbs' campaign was so strong and effective that he had another problem on his hands: the public began to see the *United States* first as a troopship and second as a luxury liner. It was almost as if that her commercial role was an afterthought.

The first public plans for the ship, which included a large-scale model (but with an extra set of aft king posts), were released at the Gibbs & Cox offices in April 1948. The project had been in the works for three years and was still subject to some modifications and changes. It was then reported that she would be 48,000 tons, over 950ft in length, carry 2,000 passengers in peace and up to 12,000 troops in war, and that she would cost $65 million. The length was soon adjusted to 980ft and finally to 990ft. The tonnage was later fixed at 53,300 and the cost increased to $70,373,000, of which the Government paid $42,285,784.

The only serious bidders to construct the new liner were Newport News and Bethlehem Steel's yard at Quincy, Massachusetts. Because of high military secrecy concerning the new ship's hull form, she had to be built in a dry dock rather than a conventional construction slip. Both yards had the facilities, but Newport News had, it would seem, the stronger relations with Government, in particular the Navy Department. That Virginia company was wildly enthusiastic upon taking on the project of the new liner and, in a news release in January 1949, reported that their two biggest drydocks would be used simultaneously for two of the world's most important ships: the new liner and the largest aircraft carrier yet constructed. The latter ship was a planned 1,090ft-long Navy aircraft carrier that would cost $124 million. She was to be called USS

United States, as the story goes, but when the order was later canceled and that project abandoned, the name was transferred over to the ship being created in the adjacent dry dock, the liner SS *United States*. The name was not revealed, however, for some time. During the keel-laying, in February 1950, without any sort of ceremony or even representation from the Government, the *New York Times* stated the ship is tentatively named *United States*.

But a huge blow crashed into all plans, on 15 September 1950, when it was announced that the *United States* and three 125-passenger combination ships under construction for American President Lines would be taken over by the Government for urgent trooping duties in the Pacific, namely for the worrisome Korean War. With her name now officially selected, disappointment that the *United States* would not now enter transatlantic liner service in the spring of 1952 was heard throughout the world. Gibbs himself was stoic. 'The *United States* was needed as a troopship and that was what she was built for,' he said from his New York offices. The ship was then 33 per cent complete and supposedly many alterations would be made in the remaining construction phases. There was also a call at the time for the need for a second superliner, one also capable of carrying up to 15,000 troops. But within six weeks, on 2 November, the Government had a change of mind. The decision was reversed and the ship would be completed as a commercial liner. No changes had been made within those six weeks and so the project continued as originally planned. By January 1952, some 3,100 workers at Newport News were working around-the-clock, on three shifts, to complete the liner. That same month, the first streams of smoke were emitted from the newly fitted funnels. Holding the aluminum structures of the giant liner together were 1.5 million aluminum rivets. But since aluminum loses strength and resistance when heated, a new process for inserting these was devised by ALCOA, the Aluminum Company of America. They were heated, then cooled and finally frozen and stored in ice cream freezers to keep them at 15 degrees below zero until hammered into place. Altogether, the welded and riveted hull required 183,000 pieces of steel, including a new type of plate, thinner but tougher than anything previously developed. This was specially produced by United States Steel. Enough material in all was used to fill a 15-mile-long freight train. Total man-hours of work on the liner would be the equivalent of constructing 6,000 average-size American homes. Earlier, Bess Truman had been asked to name the ship, but declined, supposedly on the advice of her husband, President Harry Truman, because of the division of thought within Government over whether or not to use the ship as a liner or as a troopship. Instead, the honor went to Mrs Tom Connally, wife of a Texas senator, who performed the task on an otherwise sweltering Saturday afternoon in June 1951. The ship was then floated out and moved to a fitting-out berth.

Not in fourteen years, since 1938, when Cunard's *Queen Mary* chopped out an average speed of 31.69 knots in an Atlantic crossing of 3 days, 20 hours and 42 minutes, had the mythical Blue Riband been so seriously challenged. In the spring of 1952, months before the actual maiden voyage, waterfront speculation at New York was that the *United States* would be competing for the Riband. It was already known that she was built to operate at 30 knots, but how many more knots she could make was the big question. Some felt that Chief Engineer William Kaiser would not open her up right away for, as was well known in maritime circles, power plants of ships must run for a while and be broken in before a peak load is given on a steady run. There were also rumors that the United States Lines had made a secret pact with Cunard not to try to break the record. An official at the American company later dismissed these as ridiculous. One ship, the Navy carrier USS *Lake Champlain*, had actually bettered *Queen Mary*'s record during a passage from Norfolk to Gibraltar with an average speed of 32.04 knots (4 days, 8 hours, 51 minutes), but she was not a liner and therefore ineligible as a Riband contender. There was further talk in early 1952 that the world's largest liner, the 83,673grt *Queen Elizabeth*, would have a go at the record herself. But this meant, of course, that Cunard would be outdoing itself.

The trials were an overwhelming success, but many of the actual facts and records were then kept as tight secrets. The ship raced up and down the Virginia Capes for three days. The first trials began on 14 May 1952, when the liner was about 90 per cent complete. Quickly, it was clear that she would take the Blue Ribbon with record passages, that she was free of great vibrations at high speed and that she was an excellent sea boat, comfortable, strong and solid. Called a proud present to the nation following the 175th anniversary of the signing of the Declaration of Independence, she was big news everywhere, in newspapers, magazines, new reels, on radio and on the still expanding medium of television. Her maiden voyage, scheduled for the summer of 1952, was historically timely. It had been exactly 100 years since the only other US-flagged passenger ship, the *Baltic* of the Collins Line, had taken the Ribbon. She crossed to England in 9 days and 13 hours at an average of 13.34 knots. Secretly, the Government, the shipbuilders and, of course, the United States Lines were planning for something far greater – a crossing of under 4 days and at 35 knots or even better.

The second set of trials began on 9 June and included invited passengers and official staff: some 1,700 guests, reporters and a good portion of her 1,036 crew members. These were the more dramatic tests: crash stops, full rudder tests, stability tests and an even an extraordinary stint of traveling in reverse – at 20 knots! Although many facts were still kept secret, United States Lines announced that she exceeded 34 knots, a pace surely faster than the nearest rival, the *Queen Mary*. But to a select few, the actual figure was an exceptional

The prototype of the super liner *United States* as seen by officials including William Francis Gibbs, who is just to the right of center. (Author's Collection)

39.38 knots or 241,785 total shaft horsepower (the *Queen Mary* had a maximum of 158,000, for example). In reality, she made 43 knots for a short time. Simultaneously, land sources, including the shipyard itself, said that they were probably over-estimating when putting her speed at 40 knots.

'She behaved like a fine Chris Craft', noted David Fitzgerald, one of her crewmembers and who later became her Chief Purser. The press wrote much about her, but often with less than official accuracy and comment. The number of watertight compartments onboard, for example, was not divulged. Official word was, however, that no single torpedo could sink her as one did the *Lusitania*. She could survive a collision like that which sank the ill-fated *Titanic*. Also, any fires breaking out in cargo holds could be easily controlled and put out.

In its mammoth promotional efforts, the United States Lines was allowed to address her dual engine rooms, her convertibility and her range. Each engine room had its own oil-fired boiler room driving two of the four massive propellers. A torpedo striking one engine room would disable two propellers; the other two could keep the vessel moving at a brisk clip. Previously, during the Second World War, an engine room hit would have left passenger liner-troopships helplessly adrift. On convertibility, the ship was purposely built to be stripped of commercial fittings, including cabin beds, and be fitted with bunks almost over night. In reality, she could be converted in three quick phases: for 5,000 troops on the first trip, 9,000 by the second and 14,000 by the third. As for range, it was said that the *United States* could carry a full division of troops at 10,000 miles non-stop and at better than 30 knots. Even the ship's kitchens and larders could continuously feed these 14,000 troops. Advanced air-conditioning, from the bridge to the engine room, would assure that the troops were delivered fresh and full of fight. Her owners were also proud to announce that their new flagship was 101ft wide and that, unlike both the Cunard Queens, could squeeze through the Panama Canal if needed.

Fireproofing was another subject of great attention and public interest. 'The SS *United States* couldn't possibly ever go up in flames like the *Normandie*', Gibbs noted. 'There is nothing about her to burn.' The ship was built entirely of steel, aluminum and other nonflammable materials. Only the butcher's block and two grand pianos included wood. Hand rails, deck chairs, lifeboats and all interior furniture were aluminum. The outer decks were covered with a new nonflammable material instead of the traditional teakwood. The interior decor was done in spun glass, plastics and the special fire-resistant fiber Dynel. Altogether, ninety-nine kinds of fire-retardant paint were used onboard.

The *United States* was officially handed over to the United States Lines (rather oddly, in a small office across the Hudson River, in Hoboken, New Jersey) on 20 June. Two days later, she took on 1,200 other guests who had the most prized maritime invitation of the time: to join the overnight voyage up to New York and witness the triumphant arrival into New York harbor. The *United States* reached New York for the first time and was in the news all over the world, reports sparked thoughts of a contest between the new American and Britain's *Queen Elizabeth*. On her 18 June crossing from New York to Southampton, it seems that the fourteen-year-old liner made 34 knots for a short time and that at other times was averaging just over 31 knots. It was all taken to be in preparation to rival the *United States* that same summer. Cunard dismissed the reports as 'we are merely trying to maintain our posted schedules.' With due respect, the 1,031ft-long Cunard liner did not have the reserve power to surpass the *United States*, which could, it was already reported, run with ease over 33 knots.

Every horn, whistle and siren seemed to sound as the gleaming 990-footer made her way along the Lower Bay and then along the Hudson to the north side of Pier 86. Small planes and helicopters flew overhead and fireboats let off great streams of water. Just after midday, she passed the Battery, the lower tip of Manhattan and the United States Lines offices at 1 Broadway. Minutes later, she was off 21 West Street, a slender office tower that housed the Gibbs & Cox headquarters. Flags were draped from office windows and other ships in port dressed overall in colorful flags. Salutes came from all ships at berth, especially American ones.

Some $1.3 million was spent to upgrade and redecorate 1,100ft-long Pier 86. It had been specially leased by the United States Lines, with an annual rent in 1952 of $220,000. There were celebratory luncheons, dinners and tours for the public (the proceeds of which benefitted Travelers Aid). The ship was in every newspaper across the country.

'This is the proudest day in our maritime history', declared Secretary of Commerce Charles Sawyer. He continued to say 'this ship is truly the First Lady of the Seas. No other passenger ship ever built is so beautiful, so fast, so safe, so useful.'

Expectedly, the brilliant *United States* took the record. She left a cheering New York at exactly noon on 3 July. Commodore Harry Manning was at helm and, among the 1,700 passengers, was Margaret Truman, the daughter of the President, and William Francis Gibbs himself. Two-and-a-half hours later, at 2:36, she passed the Ambrose Light, the starting point for all eastbound bids for the Blue Ribbon. On the first two days afterward, she averaged 35 knots. By the third, it was reported that she passed 36 knots. En route, she passed the French *Liberte*, herself the former German *Europa* of 1930 and a ship that held the Ribbon for three years, from 1930 until 1933. She sent greetings as did

both the *Queen Mary* and *Queen Elizabeth*. Cunard publicly announced that there would be not attempt to make a further bid for the Atlantic speed record. The *United States* officially took the Ribbon on Monday, 7 July, at just 5 in the morning. She reached Bishop Rock following a crossing of 3 days, 10 hours and 40 minutes, at an average speed of 35.59 knots. This was 3.9 knots faster than *Queen Mary*'s record made in 1938. Passengers and crew on the new American liner celebrated from stem to stern. Almost continuously, the orchestras onboard played the 'Star Spangled Banner'. Once in British waters, her reception was said to exceed even that in New York. Escort boats were said to be overloaded with many of their passengers waving tiny American flags. Even Winston Churchill sent a congratulatory telegram as did the captain of the *Queen Mary*. A long open house for the British followed at Southampton and then, on 14 July, the ship returned to New York. This was another record-making passage: 3 days, 12 hours, 12 minutes, at 34.51 knots. President Truman personally welcomed the ship at Pier 86. The inbound passenger list included Margaret Truman, Vincent Astor and Milton Berle. There was almost immediate rumor and speculation that the ship would try for a 40-knot record, but this was never in the planning. 'The great expense in doing that would be quite foolish', commented one United States Lines executive. That fall, the *United States* made her first visit to Bremerhaven, to a still weakened West Germany. By December, the ship had carried well over 90 per cent of her capacity.

Decades later, in the early 1980s, naval architect Bill Deibert recalled a conversation with a former assistant to William Francis Gibbs. Deibert was then working at the offices of Gibbs & Cox in Washington. 'I was told that the *United States* cranked up to a top speed of 43 knots during her trials and that she was belching clouds of black smoke', recalled Deibert. 'If not for the heavy smoke, she could actually have gone much faster, possibly up to 50 knots. She had these extraordinary aircraft carrier engines. But she did not have enough exhaust fan power. And, of course, the trials were a one-on situation. They were purely a maximum test. But twice as fast almost meant five times the fuel. The increments change at far different levels. And the cost quickly becomes prohibitive. Later, after her maiden voyage, her three-day record was sensibly set to a five-day standard, creating a transatlantic relay. But the great speed gave her, of course, the greatest make-up ability. She had this enormous reserve speed.'

During her first overhaul, in November 1952, the *United States* was said by Newport News engineers to be in excellent condition and needing only the most minor adjustments Hereafter, she settled down beautifully to her intended role as a transatlantic superliner, was rarely delayed, still drew large numbers on her crossings and remained impeccable. 'She will be the foremost liner in the world for the next fifty years', wrote one enthusiastic newspaper editor.

Right: The genius William Francis Gibbs. (Newport News Shipbuilding & Dry Dock Co.)

Below: The initial design of the *United States* from 1948 included, among other features, a second set of kingposts placed aft. (Cronican-Arroyo Collection)

Above: Construction is underway at Newport News in this view dated 18 August 1950. (Author Collection)

Above left: A late 1940s portrait of the liner, but which includes an aft mast that was never included. (United States Lines)

Left: Construction is well underway along the enclosed Promenade Deck. (Newport News Shipbuilding & Dry Dock Co.)

Right: The sleek, towering bow section as seen in the spring of 1952. (US Merchant Marine Museum)

Below: The top section of the forward funnel is lifted aboard. (Author's Collection)

Above: Naming the greatest liner ever to fly the American colors. (Newport News Shipbuilding & Dry Dock Co.)

Above right: After naming, the *United States* is carefully moved out of the building dock. (Cronican-Arroyo Collection)

Right: A small fleet of tugs assist the liner in this dramatic aerial view. (Cronican Arroyo Collection)

Above: In this aerial view, we can see that all the starboard davits are in place. (United States Lines)

Above right: Already majestic, imposing and certainly powerful-looking, the *United States* is moved to a fitting-out berth at the Newport News Shipyard. (Cronican-Arroyo Collection)

Right: Loading beds aboard the liner in the winter of 1952. (US Merchant Marine Museum)

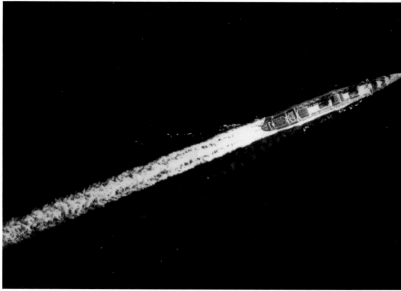

Above: The blazing sea trials of the *United States* in tests that registered up to 43 knots. (Newport News Shipbuilding & Dry Dock Co.)

Left: The great liner returns from her highly successful sea trials in May 1952. (Cronican-Arroyo Collection)

Chapter III

ROUTE OF THE 'UNRUSHABLES': TRANSATLANTIC PASSAGES

Raymond Kane joined the *United States* as a staff member in the spring of 1952. He was handpicked, after six years on the *America*, to join the new flagship and so was sent down to Newport News for the delivery. 'The United States Lines allowed forty stewards to transfer from the *America* to the *United States*', he recalled in an interview nearly fifty years later, at the New York City offices of Pisa Brothers Travel, a company he then owned.

'Before joining the *United States*, we were sent to Sheepshead Bay in Brooklyn for special training. We took courses, which included training to coxswain, which meant commanding an oar-driven lifeboat in the East River. Each of us had to receive a certificate of competence. The East River was very tough. There are terrific currents. And we had to bring the boat to a dead stop! Many of the recruits had to do the test several times over. Once aboard at Newport News, the excitement and the hard work began,' added Kane. 'The ship was absolutely pristine. There was huge publicity. Mr Gibbs and the engineers were riding up to New York. These engineers did several crossings afterward. On the way over, on the maiden voyage, I remember the chief bartender in cabin class telling me that the vibration was so great that glasses danced off the bar. A big, impromptu Conga line broke out off Bishop's Rock. I remember the Meyer Davis orchestra and, of course, Margaret Truman was aboard.'

In her first twelve months of service, the *United States* was the second-most popular liner on the Atlantic. She carried 69,231 passengers. Only the *Queen Elizabeth* was higher with 70,775 travelers while the *Queen Mary* was third at 63,443. The new American flagship, the world's fastest and safest ocean liner and the third-biggest passenger ship afloat, was a huge success. Just about

everyone wanted to sail in her, to send home post card greetings from this extraordinary, news-making craft. To sail on the *United States* was something very special, especially back in the 1950s.

'Being the world's fastest and most advanced ocean liner, and the pride of the American fleet, it was something not be missed, particularly by experienced travelers', said Alan Sherwood, who made five trips aboard that great liner beginning in 1955. 'It was like the traveling on Concorde in later years. It was exciting and you were often envied. And you talked about it for a long time afterward. The *United States* was a very, very topical and important ship. And, as an American, you were extremely proud. You always forgave or overlooked the shortcomings. She was brilliance. She was genius. She was magic!'

'The *United States* left an almost indelible impression on all who saw her. She was the most dramatic-looking ocean liner I had ever seen. Her proportions were just perfect with those two silo-sized funnels, which were wide as well as tall, and the long, very low hull,' said Robert Allan, a keen ship enthusiast, who is also an architect. He visited the *United States* for the first time in 1965, when he was seven. 'She was a ship of great proportion that also had a great sense of power and speed. The lower stern deck, for example, was a great addition to the overall look of speed. There was this great sense of slope in the stern section. The color scheme added glow and radiated the image of this immaculate, impeccably maintained moving object. The silver-painted radar mast, booms, king posts and davits added glow. I also liked the way the promenade windows lined-up with the position of the davits and the lifeboats. The *United States* was a ship of perfect planning, of perfect order.' The *United States* was one of the first ocean liners that the young Allan ever visited. His walk through the interiors, especially the passenger quarters, also left a great impression. 'The first-class dining room stands out', he remembered, 'with those brilliant red chairs and glossy black linoleum floors. It seemed then to be huge, to have a cathedral-like ceiling. The room was glowing, everything was glowing. My mother took me and was very impressed. She never seen such splendor, at least aboard a ship. She gasped at times. The Observation Lounge was another strong memory, being a room of beautiful shades of sea green and blues, and that included Venetian blinds. The metal detailing around the ship was also incredible, particularly the use of metal as a decoration. There were actual designs to give it character. Everywhere, the *United States* represented exquisite workmanship. The etched glass panels were another memory and were also quite fantastic. They were later restored and are seen today aboard the cruise ship *Celebrity Infinity*. The outer decks were better than any baseball fields I had ever seen. They were huge and so green. They were also impeccable. I remember seeing fancy-looking ladies walking about, each of them dressed like television stars with mink stoles, hats and white gloves.' Allan concluded, 'William Francis Gibbs' influence and touches were ever-present onboard as was the military connection. There were heavy bulkheads, the feeling of small compartments and that there were no vast spaces similar to those on other big liners of that time. Of course, the *United States* was very drab in many, many areas. She seemed to be all light grays and dark greens. Overall, she had a distinctly cool 1950s look.' Comparatively, the *Independence* and *Constitution*, which were built the year before but for the warmer mid-Atlantic run to and from the Mediterranean, were brighter and livelier. Noted designer Henry Dreyfuss, who decorated them, had a much softer touch.

'When thinking of the interiors, Gibbs and his associate designers were obviously very much influenced by the 1950s post-war modern architecture, which embodied a no-nonsense, plain, unadorned simplicity', noted Der Scutt, an internationally known architect. 'Design, and the pedagogy of Walter Gropius clearly and indirectly influenced the straight forward and cheerful interiors of the *United States*. Over ninety colors and shades were selected by a women's group of decorators for the interior design. Clarity, simplicity and vividness was the intended ambience. Design details added to the visual nuance.'

During this same period, the Queens were influenced by the regal interiors of London's Edwardian palaces and stately hotels. The interiors of those big Cunarders resembled also a kind of transatlantic **Deco**. Opulent trim details, lacquered floors, indirect lighting and an abundant use of wood including Maple Burr, English Elm and Ash formed the background for creamy leathers. The *United States* had no wood whatsoever and employed subtle decorative color accents of greens, blues, reds and beiges, which provided a streamlined vivacity and comfort.

'Her passenger interiors were often criticized as being too stark', remembered marine architect Bill Deibert. 'Of course, only certain fabrics could be used because of the great insistence on fire safety. But actually, materials and even designs were based on the technology of the late 1940s and so when installed, in 1951-52, they were actually three-four years behind.'

Vincent Love, a staffmember at New York, remembered the sentiments of at least one director at United States Lines' New York headquarters who was known to say that 'the *United States* had everything, but gingerbread. She was too plain!' 'Myself, I was sent to Europe on a company business trip in 1963, over on the then new *France* and home on the *United States*. I wrote a report comparing the two superliners for United States Lines and, in glaring honesty, said that the *France* was much more glamorous, had a different spirit and even was much more alive. By comparison, the *United States* was quiet, almost sedate. I also mentioned that the *France* was very stable whereas the *United States* seemed to roll a great deal. I used to watch the stacks against the sky from the top decks. Later, however, US Lines management did not take kindly to my comparisons and criticisms. The management in New York was very conservative, very dated, more reflective of the 1920s and 1930s. Someone suggested in the 1960s, as I recall, that we consider building new cargo ships in Japan. One of the directors nearly fainted. To him, it was unthinkable.'

Love added, 'by the early '60s, there were clearly design mistakes. All of the tourist class cabins lacked private facilities and this was a mistake, especially for cruising. Actually, she was a very traditional ship in ways. She tipped back to an earlier period. And, of course, she was so clean that she seemed sterile. And then there was so little carpeting in the passenger areas as another example.' Others saw the general simplicity of the *United States* in possibly more poetic terms. 'One could say that a passenger boarding the *Queen Mary* or *Queen Elizabeth* was full of anticipation for an experience of sentimental, traditional and majestic pomposity', noted Der Scutt. 'It was Cunard's celebration of classicism versus the United States Lines resplendent subtlety. One boarding the *United States* was full of excitement for an atmosphere of delicacy, tranquility, simplicity and soothing palettes. An aesthetic purity reigned, with an innovative modernist decor; a suave crispness prevailed.'

The outward appearance of the *United States* intrigued many, however. 'She always looked like a thoroughbred, a true ocean liner greyhound', added Tom Chirby, an ocean liner historian and maritime preservationist. 'She was the perfect end to a long line of Atlantic maritime behemoths. She was also the very essence of hydro-dynamic efficiency. She was also the fitting highpoint to the great career, the genius of William Francis Gibbs. Even in her current decayed and neglected state [2001], with the rust and in the solitude, her thoroughbred lines are evident. She still radiates speed, power, grace. When you see her at Philadelphia, she is unmistakable. She still plays at the imagination of many, those hoping to see her at sea again. She must be saved. She is the greatest symbol of America's great maritime might. The *United States* had this most impressive and powerful look. She looked to be in motion even when she was still at the pier.'

'I visited her a few times in the late 1960s, recalled Brad Hatry, a keen ship historian and observer. She had Tuesday-Thursday layovers at Pier 86 then and often there were midday tours on Wednesday. Decoratively, however, she was color-less and very institutional. Her biggest weakness was her interior decor. I visited at about the same time and this made for the most dramatic comparison: a floating hotel versus a floating hospital. But it was always thrilling to be on the fastest liner in the world. On the outside, she was very majestic looking. You could sense her great power. And there was something very exciting about seeing her on sailing day.'

The ship had many fans overseas as well. German marine artist Dietmar Borchert had been a longtime admirer and has often sketched and painted the American flagship. 'During much of the 1950s, Bremerhaven was the terminal port for the ship's transatlantic run', he recalled. 'Every other week or so, either the *United States* or her consort, the *America*, arrived at the Columbus Pier for their turnaround back to New York. Born in 1948, I lived with my family just a short walk from the river. In those pre-television days, we spent many Sunday afternoons promenading the dykes all the way to where the big liners berthed. You could stand on the pier and watch the ships come and go. As long as you stayed away from the bollards, the dockers never chased you away. Although I never got aboard any of the liners, at least I could get near them and take in the special atmosphere of these great ships. Often, an American troop transport would arrive and, I remember, lots of German kids would be waiting on the quayside to catch a Hershey bar, which the soldiers would throw down from the towering decks. The arrival of the SS *United States* at Bremerhaven was always a highlight', explained Borchert 'Whenever possible, I would be there early enough to watch the big ship arrive. She was the most beautiful ocean liner. She was such a sight coming in from the North Sea. Depending on the tide, she was either just slipped alongside or, arriving on an inbound tide, she would have to turn around, assisted by four or six tugs. The maneuver would take place in mid-river and so onlookers had a chance to see her broadside: long, big, sleek, spotless. She looked so fast. The raked funnels did it together with her high prow and the terraced decks aft. This impressive ship was truly an American symbol for many people. For me, she also became a measure of beauty. Since then, deciding whether the profile of a passenger ship (or cruise liner) is pleasing, I automatically compare it to the lines of the *United States*.'

The *United States* drew celebrities from all walks of life: Queen Frederika of Greece, Prince Rainier and Princess Grace of Monaco, Emperor Haile Selassie of Ethiopia, Harry and Bess Truman, Dwight and Mamie Eisenhower, Joseph Kennedy and family, Eleanor Roosevelt, Anthony Eden, Lord Mountbatten and Konrad Adenauer. And, of course, there were countless names from the world of show business who crossed her gangways. There was Ava Gardner, Mary Pickford, Greta Garbo, Joan Crawford, Cary Grant, John Wayne, Bob Hope, Errol Flynn, Marilyn Monroe, Laurence Olivier and Rex Harrison to name but a few on her passenger lists.

The Duke and Duchess of Windsor were probably the most famous, but assuredly the most loyal passengers to use the *United States*. They made over fifty crossings on the liner and always occupied the so-called Duck Suite, interconnecting first class cabins U-89, U-90 and U-91 (plus three singles across the corridor for her maid, his valet and one as a pressing room for their vast array of chic clothing). 'There was an English steward named Giles, who always served their afternoon tea in their suite', recalled Raymond Kane, then a Smoking Room steward. 'It was called the Duck Suite because of the duck wallpaper. I saw them often, on many trips. They were remote people, always very polite but always distant. They were not really interested in intermingling. They treated the staff at a distance. They did, however, always maintain a certain public persona. They were attractive people', added Kane. 'They were always beautifully groomed. She was elegant and he was a style-setter, in fact a great role model for British aristocrats. He had a certain style that included the famous Windsor Knot. I knew the bellboy, who served the Duck Suite. They used to press the button for service, various errands, something special they needed. The Duchess brought along her own bed sheets and pillow covers, which were changed each day by her own maid. But the Duchess was not alone in doing this. Mrs Harrison-Williams, for example, also brought aboard her own linens and was also served by her personal maid. The Windsors enlivened the Duck Suite with personal objects. Their pugs were allowed to stay with them and were never banished to the kennels. The Duke and Duchess attended cocktail parties and went to the dining room each evening, but had breakfast and lunch in the suite. They were looked after like royalty. United States Lines was especially proud that the ex-King of England was traveling on an American ship. It was a priceless testimonial. The Windsors were, however, not known for their public extravagance. They were well remembered as being very nominal tippers. The Windsors often had pre-luncheon and pre-dinner cocktail parties in their suite', Kane noted. There was a trolley, a portable bar, laden with all different drinks such as Manhattans, Old Fashions and Martinis. A side bar held glasses, the ice and all the ingredients. There would be fifteen to twenty fellow passengers invited. Giles personally took care of the Windsors themselves.'

'The Duck Suite was used by all the top people', recalled Raymond Kane. 'Mrs Martineau traveled in it along with a British major and two maids. She had all the pictures taken down and replaced with mirrors and special home-like lamps. Many of the first-class passengers had great eccentricities.'

Vincent Love, by then working in the so-called Conference Department at US Lines, remembered sailing with the Windsors in May 1963. 'They had a table in the Main Ballroom and I was invited to join the group that included their shipboard friends, who were all very social types. The other passengers, often dancing to the Meyer Davis orchestra, kept watching us. Myself, I felt quite special. Earlier, at Le Havre, I had met the Duke in the corridor of the boat train coming up from Paris. My first impression was that he was quite small. Proudly I thought I was taller than the King of England! The Duke had a great interest in ships and together we shared opinions and made comparisons. He felt that there was rudeness among the staff at Cunard, not only toward him for abdicating, but especially toward the Duchess. Onboard the *United States*, it was totally different, and everyone bowed and scraped, and none more so than the Americans themselves. Upon boarding, they seemed to have a lot of luggage. It seemed that every porter at Le Havre looked after them after their train arrived. They used that huge Duck Suite, which had wall covering in silver foil featuring ducks. It was created because General Franklin, the chairman of US Lines, was an avid duck hunter. The comparable suite on the other side of Main Deck was quite different done in tomato red'.

Alan Zamchick, another devoted passenger ship enthusiast, appreciated liners even in childhood. When he was twelve, he and his family were living in Europe for two years. They had gone over on the *Constitution* to Italy, where his father was employed as an exchange teacher. When it was time to return to New York, he urged his parents to take one of the big express liners, 'a real ocean liner' as he called them. 'The *United States* was not his first choice, but did become a most memorable experience. In the 1960s, living in Europe, I felt that the *United States* was a huge, metallic monstrosity. It was everything American', he noted. 'It was not like any other ship. It was very functional on the inside, no wood or brass, and of course very dual-purpose. Nonetheless, we sailed aboard her in June 1968, from Southampton via Le Havre to New York. We took the boat train down from Waterloo direct to the Ocean Terminal, which was a crate-like structure that had the feel and smell of a ship itself. It was an extension actually of the ship. There were mountains of luggage and the huge black side of the ship itself was fed by gangways. I walked aboard, seeing this black wall. I felt that big Atlantic express liners had black hulls. They were different, above all else. The all-white *Constitution* had seemed more like a cruise ship, almost a second-class liner. Before our trip, I had picked a forward-facing cabin in tourist class that I thought was outside

and therefore overlooked the bow section', said Zamchick. 'When we reached that cabin, my mistake was uncovered. There were no outside, forward-facing cabins on the *United States*. But we had a very good crossing. She was very, very fast. There was always lots of spray on deck. But she did shake a great deal and rolled and had a heavy pitch. She averaged 32 knots for the entire five days. The tourist-class public rooms were very pleasant even if she was a very sterile, very functional ship throughout. I recall seeing *The Detective* starring Frank Sinatra in the theater. My father sailed in cabin class under the Fulbright rules, but Mother and the three kids went tourist class. I felt very class conscious, especially when we passed the gates into cabin class to join my father for dinner. Nearly thirty years later, in 1997, when I visited the laid-up ship at Philadelphia, I still felt awkward when crossing the then-imaginary class separations. On our trip, there was a thick fog when we finally reached Long Island, on the approach to New York, at six in the morning. Up on deck, only one stack was visible at a time. The fog horn was blasting continuously. It was part of the great excitement of coming home.'

Zamchick visited the idle, silent and decaying liner on several occasions in the late 1990s. His walks about her stirred many emotions, memories, even some reflections. 'The *United States* will always be the Blue Ribbon queen. She should have never lost the honor, her distinction, to that tiny catamaran in 1990', he felt. 'The *United States* was in ways the perfect vessel. She never had a breakdown or a mechanical failure. She was absolutely the best-maintained ship in all maritime history. William Francis Gibbs kept her impeccable. She was also a ship of great vision, the visions of Mr Gibbs. American technology and know-how had zoomed during the Second World War and she was the embodiment of this. The only pity is that she came too late, too close to the jet era and the demise of the Atlantic liners.'

Dietmar Borchert was also a passenger aboard the US Lines flagship in the 1950s. He remembered, 'Fortune would have it that on April 4, 1958, I left Bremerhaven aboard the *United States*, bound for New York via Southampton and Le Havre. My mother and I sailed tourist class, but knowing no English yet, I had freedom of the ship. A "No Admittance – First" sign held no meaning for me. I think that I went everywhere a passenger could go without the aid of a crew member. No one ever stopped me. After we left Le Havre, it was a stormy crossing with winds up to Force 9 and 10. I soon discovered my favorite place: aft on the lowest outside deck. There was a recess, covered by the after end of the Promenade Deck. Deck chairs and blankets were stowed here and often I helped myself. Because of the stormy conditions, all outside decks were deserted. I was alone, sheltered by the deck head above, in my deck chair and covered by two or more blankets. From that position, I had a view over the stern and the horizon beyond. There was no better place to see the heaving of the big ship. I saw the gray seas disappear and then reappear, time after time, for many hours. It was something I will never, ever forget. But I also remember that I felt completely safe. One night, I fell out of my top bunk because the ship heaved so. Though unhurt, I must have stirred up a melee because the next morning some neighbors asked my mother about it. We arrived in New York on April 10th, on a cool, but sunny morning', concluded Borchert 'As the ship made her way up the Hudson, the skyline was gilded by the rising sun behind us. The big ship had hosted me for the past six days and, from what I had experienced onboard, she became something of a promise of what would lie ahead for us. I spent the next three-and-a-half years in America, the first two in New York. From my room in a Brooklyn apartment building, I had a good view over the Lower Bay and across to the naval base at Bayonne. From there, I saw all the liners come and go, almost every day of the week. Though I enjoyed the panorama immensely, I took those scenes for granted, too young then to know that all things pass. But whenever the *United States* passed by, I took extra time to watch.'

'Her passengers included corporate chieftains, families, secretaries and school teachers, the summer tourists and those Americanized immigrants returning to Europe for home visits. We also carried lots of American military passengers, actually the overflow from Military Sea Transportation Service and their peacetime troopships', added Vincent Love. 'Sometimes we would have 250 military and their families aboard and spread in all three classes. Later, in the '60s, as regular passenger loads declined, the military numbers increased. They were ideal passengers to fill the seats.'

The *United States* had a crew that numbered 1,036. To some, it was a prized, very memorable assignment; to others, it was less so. 'I can't tell you much about the *United States* other than that she was big and fast and always very clean', recalled a former steward rather apologetically. 'I was aboard her for about three years, in the early 1960s, but it was just another job. Actually, I preferred freighters.'

'There was lots of foreign help on the *United States*, but all of them were American citizens', recalled Raymond Kane. 'There were lots of Germans, some English and even a Swede at one point. The top deck stewards were either English or German. The kitchens were also English and German. The head chef was Otto Bismarck, German-born. I was the only American-born steward in the first-class smoking room. All the others were English-born. Many of the early staff on the *United States* had served on the *Leviathan*, *Manhattan* and *Washington*. In fact, in the late 1930s, there were so many Germans on the *Manhattan* and *Washington* that there were regular Bund meetings. Many of them were pro-Hitler. It became so worrisome that the FBI used to meet the ships on every arrival in 1939-40. Of course, at United States Lines, we earned much higher wages, at least twice more than those on the *Queen Mary* or *Queen Elizabeth*. And then, with overtime, it was pushed to three times more than on Cunard.'

Raymond Kane left the *United States* in 1955, after nine years with United States Lines. He concluded, 'I decided that I didn't want to spend my whole life at sea. Too many other crewmembers couldn't go ashore. Many only left the sea because the sea left them! Going to sea becomes a refuge. It becomes hard to leave. It was a great job for the income, one that exceeded almost any home job in those days, but you had to give up a personal life. I was lucky. I bought Pisa Brothers Travel in Manhattan on my savings from the United States Lines.

'The *United States* was hugely successful, sailing at over 90 per cent of her capacity on each trip', noted Daniel Trachtenberg, a former officer of the SS *United States* Preservation Foundation. But 1958, actually the first year that commercial jets flew the North Atlantic, began the slow slide, the gradual decline. The rate increased significantly in the 1960s. The jets overtook the liners such that the airlines had 95 per cent of the entire transatlantic trade by 1965.

Nicholas Bachko, the farsighted senior vice president at United States Lines, was an early and a strong proponent of modernizing the ship to be more competitive as well as become more adaptable for the growing American cruise trade. He wanted to have private facilities placed in all the tourist class cabins and to add a permanent outdoor pool. The United States Lines board was resistant, claiming to have no money, and the ever-watchful Maritime Administration objected as well. 'United States Lines knew that the *United States* was quickly becoming out of date by the late 1950s', Trachtenberg noted. 'There was also lots of strong competition coming into service, ships such as the *Rotterdam*, *Leonardo da Vinci* and *France*, to name a few. They were far better decorated and had superior amenities. Competition grew more fierce and the specific virtues of the liners were often deciding factors in choices. 'American passenger ships were not especially known for their food or their service', added Vincent Love. 'In the 1960s, the food on the *United States* was often criticized as being too American. Personally, I felt it was quite good. It was classic American fare: meat, potato and vegetables, and the likes of Baked Alaska for dessert. We used the best quality beef, for example. But the *United States* had some of the earliest microwave ovens and, after reheating, the meats never looked quite right. In fact, the beef looked gray. Overall, the service was often adequate, but not especially great. The American waiters were often said to be over-familiar, even too friendly. Even up in the first class, the service could be just fair.'

On an otherwise overcast July morning in 1959, New York harbor was

The great liner, dressed in flags from end to end and responding to seemingly endless whistle salutes, arrives in New York's Lower Bay on 23 June 1952. Over forty tugs and other harborcraft are together in the initial welcoming escort north to Pier 86. (US Merchant Marine Museum)

laying out its red carpet of welcome yet again. After the Second World War, the West German state had been penalized in many ways. One of these was not being allowed, by Allied edict, to own large passenger liners for ten years after the Nazi collapse and surrender in May 1945. Furthermore, there could be no brand-new liners built in Germany for twenty years, until after 1965. While the pre-war Hamburg American Line was not interested in resuming actual transatlantic passenger ship service (they did some supply crew members to the likes of the Home Lines and the Arosa Line, for example), the North German Lloyd did resurrect its Bremerhaven-New York passenger liner service in 1955, using the Swedish liner *Gripsholm*, built in 1925 and which had been refitted and repainted as the Lloyd-owned *Berlin*. But on that July morning, greater rebirth was occurring. A sizeable former French liner, the 30,000 ton *Pasteur*, dating from 1939, had been rebuilt and brought to luxurious standards as the

Bremen, the new pride of the reviving West German merchant marine. With fireboats spraying, added tugs in attendance and helicopters buzzing overhead, the sparkling, 699ft long *Bremen* with accommodations for 1,122 passengers in first- and tourist-class quarters – made her way along New York's Upper Bay and into the Hudson River. Ceremoniously, the smaller *Berlin* was outbound at the same time and so the two German liners passed one another at midday, just off Lower Manhattan's Battery Park. Whistles sounded and signaled. It was a proud day for the reawakening North German Lloyd. Later, as the *Bremen* – with her single, tapered, mustard-colored funnel – approached her berth at Pier 88, the *United States* was in mid-river, typically outbound from adjacent Pier 86 on a summertime crossing. Again, there was a loud exchange of greetings, good wishes and welcomes between the German and American liners. But the darkening clouds of morning soon turned to summery thunderstorms and heavy rains. They were, in ways, hints of the dramatic changes unfolding on the North Atlantic passenger run. Just nine months before, the first jet aircraft with passengers had crossed between New York and London. Ocean liner history quietly rattled, even if Cunard, in deep wonderment, announced that flying was merely a passing fad. Indeed, it was anything but a fad. It was the new, technological wonder and which both fascinated as well as appealed to the traveling public.

And so, as the *Bremen* was docking for the first time and the *United States* was outbound on another six-night run to Le Havre, Southampton and Bremerhaven, the airlines had already secured two-thirds of all Atlantic travelers. It was a swift, merciless end to the Atlantic liner. Quite simply, it was all just a matter of time. None other than the captain of the *Queen Mary* reflected, 'I didn't realize it, but it was all over.' Decline and withdrawal were clearly evident when, in the fall of 1964, the *America* was retired and sold off. Thereafter, the *United States* was alone, still notable, enduring, but struggling. And the fates were sometimes against her. In 1965, she was very hard hit by a long seamen's strike, which included the cancellation of her peak summer season sailings. Desolate and looking quite lonely, she sat along the north side of Pier 86 as a new, flashier generation of Atlantic liners such as the *France*, *Michelangelo* and *Raffaello* inherited her passengers. But some fleetmates began leaving the diminishing Atlantic stage. The venerable *Queen Mary*, faded, rusting and uneconomic, was withdrawn by the historic, very traditional Cunard Line in September 1967 and then the *Queen Elizabeth* followed thirteen months later, in October 1968. The American Export sisters *Independence* and *Constitution* were yanked from service as well.

There are thick stacks of memos in the United States Lines archives suggesting that the *United States* be re-invented as a cruise ship by the early 1960s. Some company executives wanted more and more cruises, from short hops to Bermuda to three-months around-the-world. Many at the Lower

Broadway head office felt that she should be a cruise ship for six months each year. When she finally did begin to make a few, off-season cruises, the entire tourist-class section had to be closed off because none of the cabins had facilities. Private bathrooms were cherished by Americans, especially those on a vacation cruise. She failed, however, in her comparison to the likes of the *France* and the brand new *Oceanic* (1965), onboard which every cabin had at least a private shower and toilet. Even Cunard saw the writing on the wall and spent millions by modernizing the twenty-five-year-old *Elizabeth* in 1965. Among other features, that giant ship was fitted with complete air-conditioning and a large, after-deck pool.

The first cruise for the *United States*, a two-week jaunt around the sunny Caribbean, left Pier 86 in January 1962. The ship's great fame made it a success. For many not wanting to go to Europe, it was a chance to sail on the world's fastest liner and certainly one of the most acclaimed.

'These cruise voyages took tremendous advance planning, often more than a year in advance', noted Daniel Trachtenberg. 'Small teams were sent ahead to check ports, their docks, tender facilities, tide schedules, tug services and the length of stay needed. The *United States* was given a portable, canvas-style pool for these warm weather trips. This pool was actually shared with the *America* at the beginning and used when she cruised. A detailed schedule was arranged for it at the United States Lines cargo offices on Pier 62. Onboard the *United States*, there was always a pool opening ceremony every cruise. It was positioned on the raised tennis court aft and placed on the neo-tech decking. The company even tried plastic palm trees and colored balloons, but it was all a rather weak attempt to make her a tropic cruiser.

'We actually started off-season, mostly wintertime cruising with the *America* in 1961', added Vincent Love. 'From the head office, these cruise passengers seemed quite ordinary. They even carried their own canapes aboard on sailing day. Actually, it all seemed a big come down for US Lines and their Atlantic crossings. But the company had no other choice. We had been carrying 10 per cent of all transatlantic passengers – 100,000 out of the 1 million in 1958 – but the numbers were dropping quickly, especially by 1961. And our operating costs were moving up into the stratosphere. But we had our own limits with cruising. Onboard the *United States*, we could not use tourist class since all of the cabins were without private bathroom facilities. Consequently, her capacity for cruises was placed at approximately 1,200.'

Love added, 'She stopped making money in about 1961-62, although this was a well-kept secret at the time. And unfortunately, the cruises were not highly profitable because of the reduced capacity. It seemed that every cruise passenger wanted to be in the first-class restaurant and that wasn't possible.'

The ship plowed on in the often turbulent, very uncertain 1960s. Her roughest crossing was said to have been in January 1961, when crusted with ice, she reached Pier 86 twenty-four hours late. 'It was surely her worst crossing yet', noted Captain John Anderson, her master. 'With 915 passengers aboard, she encountered hurricane-force winds of more than 75 miles an hour. These winds and 60ft-high waves twice forced the liner to heave to. During one day, her speed was cut from 31 to 16 knots and winds buckled two doors on the Main Deck.

On 1 July 1962, the *United States* departed for Europe with 1,755 passengers aboard, a peak summer crossing. It was her tenth anniversary. As she steamed along the Hudson and then into the Lower Bay, it was announced that she had clocked some 1,605,000 miles and all without a single breakdown or mishap. There were few recorded delays, other than those caused by strikes, in her 226 round trips (or 454 crossings) and, by then, two winter Caribbean cruises. She had carried 653,638 passengers at an average of 88.5 per cent of her capacity. She was then costing over $20 million to operate, a third of which went to wages for her crew. Some $3.5 million was spent on fuel, $3.3 million for repairs and $1.3 million for maintenance. Annual insurance cost $1 million, port and cargo handling charges amounted to $2.4 million and commissions to travel agents came to $1 million. Another $1 million went to crew benefits. She was also a great source of revenue to local New York suppliers. Before a typical departure from Pier 86 on a five-day crossing to Europe, she took on the likes of 58,580 pounds of dry stores, 61,025 pounds of dairy foods, over 13,000 pounds of fish and some 32,100 pounds of fresh vegetables. Other items on the ship's shopping list included 37,000 pounds of fresh fruit, 59,200 pounds of meat and 22,000 pounds of potatoes. There was also three tons of ice cream and, especially for *bon voyage* parties, a ton of ice cubes. Fifteen tons of beer also went aboard.'

Myself, I well recall a misty summer's evening in the early 1960s when, quite unusual to her normal scheduling of midday departures, the *United States* proceeded down the Hudson in the last light of day. She had departed from Pier 86, as many of her passengers had already finished with dinner rather than lunch, almost eight hours late. There had been a short strike. The all-powerful American seamen's unions were unhappy and so flexing their firm muscle over the 1,000 crewmembers and over the United States Lines.

Of course, the liner looked stunning – her huge funnels already lighted, her portholes and promenade windows aglow and, forming a backdrop in the stage set, the Manhattan skyline was already beginning to twinkle and glow. With that extraordinary ease and sense of purpose, her own Yankee majesty, the *United States* could not have looked more beautiful. But times and indeed those good old days for *United States* were changing rapidly. In a feature story of the 1 September 1968 edition of the *New York Times*, it was revealed that

United States had finally been declassified by the both the Government and her operators, the United States Lines. In a decision made fifteen days earlier, on 15 August, the Navy Department added that there was simply no reason to be secretive any further. The liner was described as the most over-designed merchant ship ever to emerge from draftsman and builder. Photographs were also released of her never-before-seen underwater hull, her engine rooms and her four propellers. It was publicly announced that she could make up to 42 knots. It was also noted that if all boilers were in use, the 990ft long liner would consume 12,000 barrels of oil per day. But under normal operations, at a speed of 30 knots, she burned 5,400 barrels a day. There were about sixty different compartments onboard for carrying fuel, but some of them had never been used for anything except salt-water ballasting. Indeed, she could go around-the-world without refueling. The concept of numerous fuel tanks was part of the original defense features of the ship. The layout of her tanks and their duplication meant that, in time of war, she could continue sailing even after several hits.

The forward engine room, it was revealed, ran the two, five-bladed outboard propellers while the aft engine room handled the two, four-bladed inboard props. Speculation developed on her speed if forced to use only one engine room. Nicholas Bachko, then chairman of the United States planning committee and who was a project engineer for two years during her construction, was reluctant to discuss such a possibility, but finally said, 'perhaps as much as 27 or 28 knots on two props'. Bachko also recalled the record-breaking maiden voyage. 'The *United States* performed all the dreams of her designers, builders and operators. Her record in July 1952 of 3 days, 10 hours and 40 minutes was better than we ever expected. But we were taking no chances on that highly publicized first crossing. For that trip, every inch of her underwater hull had been sandpapered by hand to eliminate even the slightest chance of extra drag.'

The question of fire safety was also addressed by Bachko. 'Mr Gibbs always boasted that the ship was so fireproof that the only wood onboard was in the pianos and the butcher blocks. Actually, there was wood in one other place. The broad bilge keels that stick out from her sides for stability are about 4ft wide and about 200ft long. They are of relatively light metal, but their interiors are packed with balsa wood. Of course, they are outside the ship, unreachable by fire.'

The liner's engine rooms were opened for the first time for passenger tours and inspections in September 1968, but almost too late. Within fourteen months, the ship would be abruptly removed from service. Those great engine rooms, like all else onboard, would soon be silent, and seemingly forever. Ironically, in September 1968, on a voyage following delays caused by yet another seamen's strike, the *United States* showed her true colors and kicked up her heels, making her most remarkable speed since the records of 1952. She averaged 33.06 knots on the five-day run between New York, Le Havre and Southampton. She made up time lost in the short strike, returned to her posted schedule and on the return was able, as United States Lines reported, to return to a much more leisurely 30 knots . Shortly before, Chief Engineer William Kaiser reported that, 'She is better than ever, mostly because of the outstanding maintenance and care we have lavished on her.' He concluded his praises, 'We can still do up to 22.7 knots going astern – or more than the average liner going ahead.'

Fred Rodriguez was a bellman aboard *United States* for four of her last voyages, in the summer and fall of 1969. 'She was still very well maintained. She shined everywhere, even after seventeen years of service. Even the crew areas were immaculate. But she was always short of crew by then. Just about anyone could get a job on her, but through the Seamen's Union, of course. Actually, there were lots of college students working aboard during the summer months and so there would always be lots of parties in the crew areas. The crew lived in cabins with two to ten berths. At sea, the *United States* rode very well', added Rodriguez. 'She went straight through Hurricane *Camille* and not around it. We were on a voyage to New York from Le Havre, Southampton and Bremerhaven and had two days of very stormy weather. But she kept her speed. Storm lines were everywhere, however. The porthole in my small, forward cabin looked like a window in a washing machine and all while there was solid, continuous pounding. I was scared and sick for two full days, turned an awful green and vowed never to return to the sea. The hurricane lingered right up to the Verrazano-Narrows Bridge. She was filled to capacity on that return trip. She had lots of troops and their families going from Bremerhaven to New York. Most of them were in tourist class. The bellmen all made extra money by babysitting for these military families. On later trips, I became a first-class bellman and made much better tips. The combined tips were sometimes more than the actual wages. I had been fascinated by the *United States* since I was eight years old, in 1956', he added. 'I built the Revell model of her. She was a fascinating ship in every way, and I especially loved those big red, white and blue funnels. Years later, in the mid-1960s, I did a painting of the ship and wrote to Commodore Alexanderson. He invited me to come aboard and present it. In 1969, when I was working aboard, I wrote a note to the Commodore, who was still in command, and he invited me up to a passenger cocktail party. He insisted I wear my uniform, however. Afterwards, he presented me with a United States Lines bottle-opener as a souvenir.'

Right: No less than five Moran tugs assist with the docking at Pier 86. (United States Lines)

Above left and right: Ocean liner buff John McFarlane especially traveled to Pier 86, at the foot of West 46 Street, to witness the first arrival of the new American super liner. As she is turned into the slip, more and more of the liner's sleek lines come into view and as he created a series of first arrival photos. (John McFarlane Collection)

Her 990ft length is here being positioned between Piers 86 and 88, the latter belonging to the French Line. (John McFarlane Collection)

Now too large for his camera frame, the docking is almost complete. (John McFarlane Collection)

Left: One of the world's most beautiful liners – *United States* prepares to sail from Pier 86, New York.

Above left and right: High spirits! The great liner arrives at New York for the first time (left) and then sails off at 12 noon (right) on 3 July 1952 on her record-breaking maiden crossing to Southampton and Le Havre. (United States Lines)

Left: Enthusiast John McFarlane was back at Pier 86 on the afternoon of 3 July for the gala sendoff. (John McFarlane Collection)

Above left: Outbound for Europe and passing the Lower Manhattan skyline. (United States Lines)

Above right: Passing Lower Manhattan. (United States Lines)

Above left: Triumphant, the *United States* arrives at Le Havre on the evening of 7 July, having crossed the Atlantic in record-breaking time: 3 days, 10 hours and 40 minutes. (Cronican-Arroyo Collection)

Above right: The *United States* outward bound, in Southampton Water, July 1952. (J&C McCutcheon Collection)

Right: Luggage is unloaded onto the *United States* from two Hills of Southampton trucks in this late 1950s view by Judges of Hastings. (J&C McCutcheon Collection)

Having won the Blue Riband, the victorious *United States* arrives in New York's Lower Bay on 15 July 1952 following her first roundtrip crossing. (United States Lines)

John McFarlane returned to Pier 86 on the morning of 15 July to witness the great ship's dazzling return. (John McFarlane Collection)

Above left: The *United States* made headlines not only in the USA, but around the world. Here we see the cover of *Newsweek* magazine, dated 30 June 1952. (Rich Romano Collection)

Above right: A full-page advertisement for the maiden season of the *United States*. (Rich Romano Collection).

Above left: Berthing at Southampton in 1952 with three tugs pushing *United States* into her berth in the Western Docks. (J&C McCutcheon Collection)

Above right: Wintery morning: the *United States* arrives in the ice-filled Hudson River in this view dated 1959. (Charles Howland Collection)

Left: August 1952 and the *United States* enters Southampton Water on her fifth voyage. (J&C McCutcheon Collection)

Right: In a most unusual occurrence, the *United States* is berthed on the south side of Pier 86. (Charles Howland Collection)

Above: The grand ship at sea. (Newport News Shipbuilding & Dry Dock Co.)

Right: A noon departure as seen from the open-air veranda at the end of Pier 86. (Charles Howland Collection)

Above left: The *United States*, the *America* and the Italian *Andrea Doria* at the New York piers in 1955. (Gillespie-Faber Collection)

Above right: The great liner sails past midtown Manhattan with the Empire State Building to the right. (United States Lines)

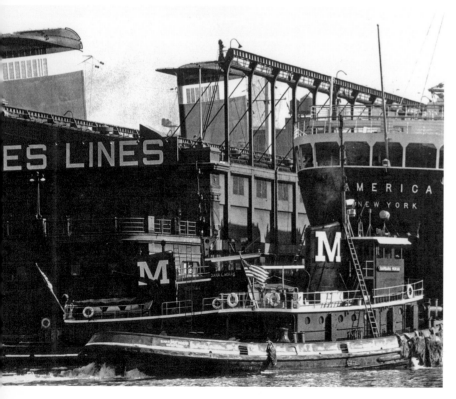

Left: Moran tugs attend to the *America* in this 1964 photo and with the two enormous funnels of the *United States* resting above the pier shed. (Frank O. Braynard Collection)

Above left: Towering above the tug *Kerry Moran*, the *United States* prepares for another outbound sailing to Europe. (Moran Towing & Transportation Co)

Above right: The author at age seventeen visiting aboard the *United States* prior to a February 1966 departure. (Author's Collection)

Departure from New York in a view dated 1966.
(Norman Knebel Collection)

Inward bound to Southampton and with five
tugs bringing her in, on 20 July 1966. (J&C
McCutcheon Collection)

Well-wishers see off the liner in this scene dated September 1967. (Author's Collection)

Smoke-filled departure as the *United States* gets away on a Saturday afternoon in the summer of 1968. (Author's Collection)

Opposite, clockwise from top left:
Boyhood dreams! Ship enthusiast Pine Hodges as a young boy of ten as he visits Luxury Liner Row at New York in July 1969. (Pine Hodges Collection)

Summer dreams! Young Pine and his brother look toward the Hudson River as the great liner begins her voyage. (Pine Hodges Collection)

The brothers see almost the full length of the 990ft-long *United States*, which is framed between Piers 86 and 88. (Pine Hodges Collection)

Berthed in Luxury Liner Row, July 1969. (Pine Hodges Collection)

Above: Outbound, the *United States* at speed on her first transatlantic crossing. (J&C McCutcheon Collection)

Passing Lower Manhattan in this view dated 11 August 1958. (Port Authority of New York & New Jersey)

Passing the Battery, the tip of Manhattan island. (Rich Romano Collection)

Above left: Arriving at Southampton with the classic *Queen Mary* berthed at the Ocean Terminal in the background. (United States Lines)

Above right: Another arrival at Southampton. (Richard Faber Collection)

Right: Passing Calshot, Southampton, on her record-breaking maiden voyage, the *United States* is dressed overall in flags for the occasion. (J&C McCutcheon Collection)

THE "UNITED STATES" PASSES CALSHOT.

Above left: With her decks aglow and her funnels floodlit, the *United States* makes for a very glamorous set piece in this view at the Ocean Terminal at Southampton. (United States Lines)

Above right: Departure from Le Havre with *Batory* of the Polish Ocean Lines on the left and the *France* of the French Line to the right. (Port Authority of Le Havre)

An aerial view at Le Havre. (Richard Faber Collection)

Right: Inbound to her pier in New York in the late 1950s, The *United States* is nudged in by a Moran tug. (J&C McCutcheon Collection)

Below left: A crowd watches as the *United States* is berthed at the Columbus Quay in Bremerhaven. (J&C McCutcheon Collection)

Below right: Passing the breakwater at Le Havre. (United States Lines)

Left: Bon Voyage! Crowds see off the *United States* at Bremerhaven. (Richard Faber Collection

Below: Berthed at the Columbus Quay at Bremerhaven. (Alvin E. Grant Collection)

Right: Tugs attend to the liner in the river at Bremerhaven. (Alvin E. Grant Collection)

Below: Three classic American liners at New York in a view dated 2 October 1958. The *Constitution* is to the left with the *America* in the center and the *United States* on the right. But both the *America* and *United States* are strike-bound and their European crossings have been cancelled. (Cronican-Arroyo Collection)

Above left: High summer along Luxury Liner Row! In a view from 4 September 1957, there are the *Britannic*, *Queen Mary* and *Mauretania* of Cunard; the *Flandre* of French Line; the *Olympia*, Greek Line; the *United States*; and *Independence* of American Export Lines. (Port Authority of New York & New Jersey)

Above right: Wintery afternoon: the brand new *France* is in mid-Hudson, departing on her eastbound maiden voyage while (from left to right) the *Cristoforo Colombo* of Italian Line as well as the *America* and *United States* are at dock. (Cronican-Arroyo Collection)

Left: Teammates: the *America* and *United States* so often shared Pier 86. (United States Lines)

Early morning arrival: the *United States* sails into Pier 86 with the *Cristoforo Colombo* and the *Queen Mary* farther down river. (Author's Collection)

Marine artist Don Stoltenberg created a series of superb paintings of the *United States*. (Stoltenberg Collection)

Above left: Classic scene: the outbound *America* passes the inbound *United States* in this view from 1952. (Newport News Shipbuilding & Dry Dock Company)

Above right: North German Lloyd's *Bremen* arrives on her maiden voyage at New York in this July 1959 view. Just behind, the *United States* is outbound. (Author's Collection)

Right: Another dramatic Stoltenberg scene of the liner, now in the collection of Thomas Cassidy. (Don Stoltenberg)

High glamor! The *United States* is seen in this night-time view of midtown Manhattan. North German Lloyd's *Europa* is to the left. (Author's Collection)

Passing the Chargeurs Reunis berths at Le Havre. (J&C McCutcheon Collection)

Left: Early morning arrivals: the *Independence* and *United States* are inbound in this scene dated 15 September 1961. (Fred Rodriguez Collection)

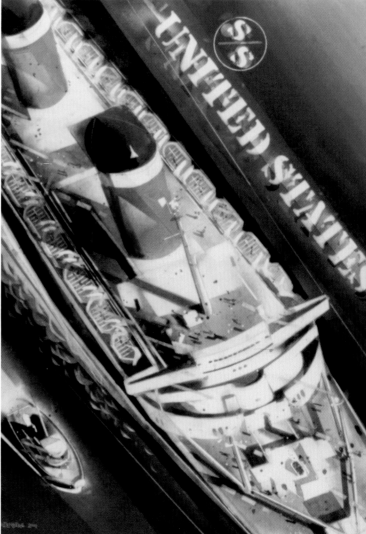

Right: A commemorative painting by Don Stoltenberg of the liner and created in 2001. (Don Stoltenberg)

This page: Luggage tags from *United States*. (J&C McCutcheon Collection)

Left: Inside the world's fastest liner: The oval-shaped first-class Ballroom. (Cronican-Arroyo Collection)

Right: Festivity! Passengers in costume parade in the ballroom during a wintertime Caribbean cruise. (Charles Howland Collection)

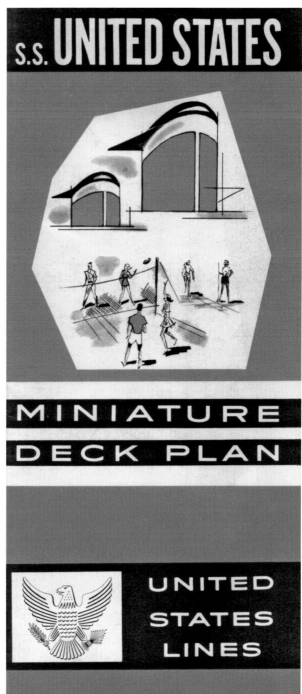

This page: Two deckplans given away to prospective passengers, the first from March 1957 and the second from the mid-1960s. (J&C McCutcheon Collection)

Left: A 1993 Stoltenberg painting of the American flagship. (Don Stoltenberg)

Below: The first-class Writing Room. (Cronican-Arroyo Collection)

Left: The splendor of the first-class Dining Room. (Cronican-Arroyo Collection)

Right: Fine dining afloat – an officer's table during an Atlantic crossing in the 1960s. (Charles Howland Collection)

Another view of the first-class Dining Room. (Cronican-Arroyo Collection)

The ship's theater. (Cronican-Arroyo Collection)

Above left: The first-class Smoking Room. (Cronican-Arroyo Collection)

Above right: 1950s modernity, cabin M58 in first class with bedroom and sitting area. (Cronican-Arroyo Collection)

Right: The sitting room of a large first-class suite, which also consisted of two large bedrooms, three baths and dressing and trunk rooms. (US Merchant Marine Museum)

Above left: The popular indoor swimming pool. (Cronican-Arroyo Collection)

Above right: The cabin-class Smoking Room. (Cronican-Arroyo Collection)

Left: In-cabin entertaining before dinner. (Charles Howland Collection)

Above: The Main Lounge in cabin class. (Cronican-Arroyo Collection)

Right: Tourist-class deck plan from 1952. (J&C McCutcheon Collection)

Below: The Cabin Lounge is a large, colourful room surrounded on both sides by the covered Cabin promenade deck. Aluminum leaf glazed to a pink-beige covers the walls. (J&C McCutcheon Collection)

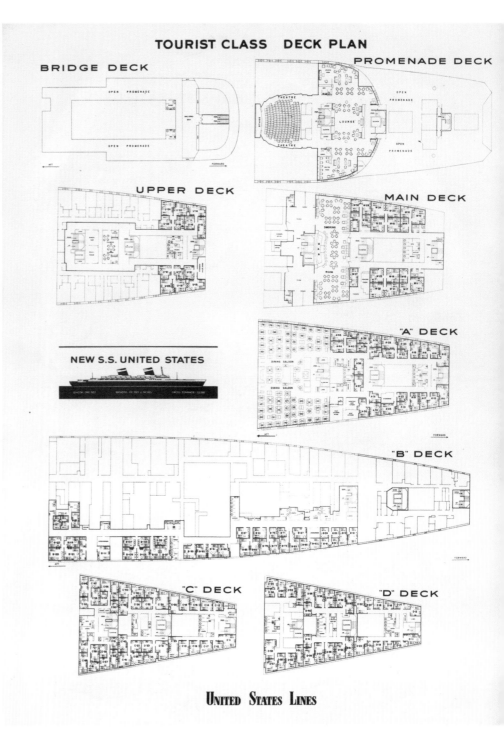

Above left: The tourist-class Main Lounge. (Cronican-Arroyo Collection)

Above right: The tourist-class Dining Room. (Cronican-Arroyo Collection)

Above: Count on fun in the Tourist Lounge. It's the place for daytime or evening get-togethers ... (J&C McCutcheon Collection)

Left: The tourist-class Smoking Room. (Cronican-Arroyo Collection)

Above: Shown as a three-berth room, this tourist-class cabin has an added fourth berth, but which is concealed against the upper wall on the left. (US Merchant Mariner Museum)

Right: The liner at sea seen from the starboard side docking bridge. (United States Lines)

Below: The Tourist staterooms are extremely cheerful and comfortable. (J&C McCutcheon Collection)

Above: An extra-special treat for Tourist passangers is a modern theater all their own. (J&C McCutcheon Collection)

Left: A late afternoon view of the stern section. (United States Lines)

Opposite, clockwise from top left:
Deck tennis anyone? (Charles Howland Collection)

Enjoying the fresh sea air! (Charles Howland Collection)

By the 1960s, as jets roared across the Atlantic, voyages onboard the *United States* were advertised as the route of the unrushables. Comfort and relaxation were emphasized as part of a grand sea voyage. (United States Lines)

Enjoying mild weather on a five-day summer crossing. (Cronican-Arroyo Collection)

Left: Sunset off the stern during a summertime crossing. (United States Lines)

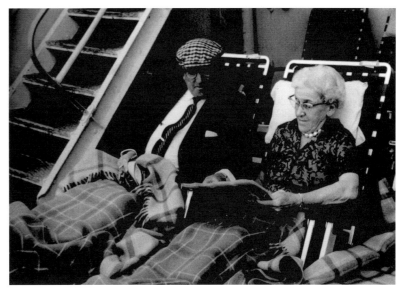

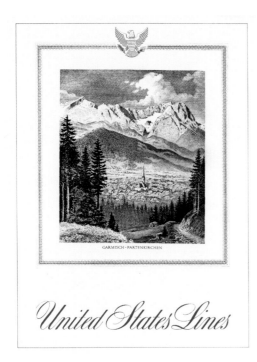

GARMISCH - PARTENKIRCHEN

United States Lines

THE GIANT SEQUOIA TREES

United States Lines

THE HALF MOON

Breakfast

FRUITS
Chilled Cantaloupe
Chilled Spanish or Honeydew Melon   Sliced Banana with Cream
Frozen Strawberries with Cream   Frozen Peaches in Syrup
Melon Balls   Sliced Fresh Pineapple or Orange   Baked Apple
Fresh Fruit Salad   Iced Grapefruit   Fresh Grapes
Preserved Fruits: Figs in Syrup, Cherries, Peaches or Kumquats
Stewed Fruits: Apricots, Prunes, Pears or Mixed Fruit
Juices: Pineapple, Grape, Tomato, Apple, Prune,
Orange, Vegetable, Grapefruit, Sauerkraut or Clam

CEREALS
Boiled Cream of Wheat with Milk
H-O Oats with Milk   Strained Porridge   Kellogg's Special "K"
Grape-Nut Flakes   Shredded Wheat   Corn Flakes   Bran Flakes 40%
Pep   Grape-Nuts   Sugar-Frosted Flakes   Sugar Pops   Pablum
Puffed Wheat   Raisin Bran   Rice Krispies   Puffed Rice   Cocoa Krispies

FISH
Findon Haddie Flakes in Double Cream   Broiled Bloater Herring
Broiled Kippered Herring, Melted Butter   Porgie, Sauté Meunière

EGGS
Boiled   Poached   Shirred   Buttered   Fried with Ham or Bacon
Scrambled: à l'Écarlate, Onions, Green Peas, Shrimps, Mushrooms or Plain
Omelettes: Chicken Hash, Spanish, aux Confitures, Asparagus Tips or Plain

MEATS
Chicken Liver, Sauté, Sauce Madeira   Kusch Kusch, Pan Gravy

FROM THE GRILL
Chopped Sirloin Steak   Single Lamb Chop on Toast   Small Breakfast Steak
Ham: Prague or Sugar-cured Yorkshire   Palethorpes or Country Sausages
Bacon: American Breakfast, Wiltshire or Canadian

Potatoes: Boiled, Mashed or Lyonnaise

Cold Dishes: Lachs Ham   Sliced Breast of Chicken
Beef Steak, Tartare   **Cheese:** Swiss or Boursin
Various Kinds of Fresh and Smoked German Sausages

Wheat or Buckwheat Griddle Cakes with Maple or Coconut Syrup
Vanilla Waffles   Croissants   Zwieback   Bagels   English Muffins
Currant Buns   Scotch Scones   Rye Crisp   Sweet Buns
White Rolls   French, Melba, Buttered or Dry Toast

PRESERVES
Jams: Blackberry, Raspberry, Strawberry, Cherry, Apricot, Damson, Peach
or Plum   Comb or Strained Honey   Lime or Orange Marmalade
Jellies: Red Currant, Guava, Strawberry or Bar le Duc (Red)   Preisselbeeren

BEVERAGES
Coffee: American, Nescafé, Sanka, Instant Sanka, Mocha or Kaffee Hag
Teas: English Breakfast, Ming Cha, Orange Pekoe, Darjeeling, Green, Oolong
Homogenized Milk, Skimmed Milk, Buttermilk or Yogurt
Cocoa, Chocolate, Instant Chocolate, Ovaltine or Postum

WB—FCBr-IV   **Sunday, April 1, 1962**

UNITED STATES LINES

This page: Typical menu covers as used throughout the lifetime of the *United States*. (J&C McCutcheon Collection)

Above: 'Come on in the water's fine!' That's the happy invitation spelled out by the pennant flags at the far end of this brightly-coloured Swimming Pool. Electric stars sparkle on the water ... lounging chairs line the water's edge under gayly-striped awnings. (J&C McCutcheon Collection)

Right: A poetic afternoon view at sea. (Frank O. Braynard Collection)

Below: An artist depiction of the liner at the Ocean Terminal at Southampton. (Author's Collection)

Above left: Customs and luggage-handling at the Ocean Terminal. (United States Lines)

Above right: The late marine artist Frank Braynard's sketch of the outer decks aboard the *United States*. (Frank O. Braynard Collection)

Left: A typically posed publicity photograph during an Atlantic crossing. (Charles Howland Collection)

Above: Her Majesty Queen Frederika of Greece arrives at New York in 1958 aboard the American flagship. (United States Lines)

Right: Actor John Wayne on the starboard bridge of the liner with Commodore John Anderson. (United States Lines)

Above left: Sailing day at New York: from left to right, actor David Janssen and his wife, then film stars Cyd Charise and Tony Martin. (United States Lines)

Above right: The Duke and Duchess of Windsor were perhaps the most publicized passengers onboard the *United States*. (Author's Collection)

Left: The sitting room of the Duck Suite, always used by the Duke and Duchess of Windsor. (United States Lines)

Above: The Windsors celebrating their wedding anniversary aboard the liner in a photo dated 3 June 1967. (United States Lines)

Right: Film queen Joan Crawford meets reporters before sailing for Europe. (United States Lines)

Above left: Shipyard crews prepare to moor the liner, a mooring line having just been thrown from her bow. (Newport News Shipbuilding & Dry Dock Co.)

Above right: The *United States* as seen through a wheelhouse window of a Newport News tugboat as she arrives at the shipyard for her winter dry docking. (Newport News Shipbuilding & Dry Dock Co.)

Above: Early morning: the *United States* is being handled by tugs as she arrives at the Newport News Shipyard for her annual overhaul. (Charles Howland Collection)

Right: A shipyard pilot boards the mighty ship. (Newport News Shipbuilding & Dry Dock Co.)

Above: Shipyard crews receive the first lines from the *United States* as she arrives at Newport News. (Newport News Shipbuilding & Dry Dock Co.)

Above right: Mooring lines are being set in place. (Newport News Shipbuilding & Dry Dock Co.)

Above left: A tug assists in the final docking. (Newport News Shipbuilding & Dry Dock Co.)

Above right: Slowly and carefully, the 990ft-long liner is positioned within the graving dock. (Newport News Shipbuilding & Dry Dock Co.)

Right: View from the bridge of the liner as she enters dry dock at Newport News. (Newport News Shipbuilding & Dry Dock Co.)

Above left: The graving dock is being flooded in this view as the liner begins her three-week winter overhaul. (US Merchant Marine Museum)

Above right: The great bow within the graving dock. (Newport News Shipbuilding & Dry Dock Co.)

Left: An aerial view of the ship entering the graving dock. (Newport News Shipbuilding & Dry Dock Co.)

Above left: Another view of the *United States* during her winter dry docking, dated 1955. (Cronican-Arroyo Collection)

Above right: On another occasion at Newport News Shipyard, the *United States* is seen here to the left of the nuclear-powered aircraft carrier USS *Enterprise*. (United States Lines)

Left: The liner is in the so-called wet dock at Newport News with the carrier USS *Forrestal* to the right in this 1955 view. (US Merchant Marine Museum)

Above left: A stern view of the liner and the *Enterprise*. (United States Lines)

Middle: Of course, the great funnels need cleaning and repainting as well. (Newport News Shipbuilding & Dry Dock Co.)

Above right: Commodore Leroy J. Alexanderson, the last master of the *United States*. (United States Lines)

Chapter IV

THE LONG SLEEP

'There had been lots of rumors that the ship would be withdrawn during 1969', explained crew member Fred Rodriguez. But many were still confident that she had another year. Some even said she had several years more. The *Independence* and *Constitution* had just been pulled out of service by the money-losing American Export Lines passenger division in 1968, and Moore-McCormack Lines had abruptly decommissioned their *Argentina* and *Brasil* in September 1969. And the future of the Grace Line passenger fleet was slipping into further uncertainty as well. On the West Coast, Matson Line was pulling out of liner service (by June 1970), and would sell off the *Lurline* to the Greeks and sisters *Mariposa* and *Monterey* to the Pacific Far East Line. American President Lines was downsizing as well. The *President Roosevelt* would join the *Lurline* in Greek hands. Concurrently, there was talk that ships like *United States* would become fulltime cruise ships, sail for other American owners and might even raise a less costly, foreign flag, say Panama or Liberia. Then there was also a rumor that the Navy wanted her for use as an accommodation ship.

In fact, *United States* Voyage 400 in November 1969 proved to be the end. Generally, there had been something of a decline. Maintenance was still impeccable and the ship run to an exacting, if somewhat accelerated schedule, but the mood had changed and prospects for the future looked grim. Edgar Macey, the ship's baggage master since the maiden voyage seventeen years earlier, actually quit the United States Lines in June 1969, five months before she was abruptly and unexpectedly decommissioned. In later years, he said, 'I began to see cutbacks, many cutbacks, onboard the *United States*. Things were not the same. I even saw passengers carrying their own bags on occasion.'

'The mood at US Lines passenger offices in Lower Manhattan by 1968-69 was declining as well. Her numbers were going down and there were increasing labor troubles, while wages were soaring and we had the likes of automatic elevators still being run by well-paid operators', remembered Vincent Love. 'We heard lots of rumors, beginning that summer, but which only increased by November 1969. We were optimistic, however. The ship was scheduled for her first world cruise, Around the World in 80 Days, departing in January 1970. It was heavily booked and the New York office staff were planning to join on various segments. But as she sailed on that autumn night (7 November), we watched from a Lower Manhattan pierhead. She was all aglow, those huge stacks illuminated. The whistles sounded off the Battery. That day, we had heard the strongest rumors that the end was near. Shortly after, it was all confirmed. She was finished. We would never see her in New York harbor again. And within a month, I lost my job after ten years with United States Lines. She had arrived from Europe and was at Pier 86 prior to going down to Newport News for her annual overhaul.'

'She was due back in December for some cruises and further crossings', remembered Fred Rodriguez. 'I had gone down to Pier 86 to take some night photos of the ship. I went aboard and wandered up to the bridge, knowing that she was sailing for Virginia at 9 o'clock. I met Commodore Alexanderson, but he became alarmed. The ship was sailing immediately, at 8 o'clock instead. He called to have one gangway held. I flew off. Later, I went out on a Moran tug. Those great whistles on the *United States* blew. She was lighted from end to end, like a glowing birthday cake. There was no ceremony, no crowd of well-wishers, no committee from the United States Lines. Except for the longshoremen on Pier 86, there wasn't a soul in sight. That was the last time she was in New York. She sat idle, dark and lonely at the Newport News Shipyard until moved, in the following June, to a nearby finger pier at Norfolk. Three years later, she was officially transferred to the US Government, to the Maritime Administration. Thirteen large humidifers were placed aboard and kept the otherwise empty ship airtight. Rumors mounted with the years. It was said she would be revived as a cruiseship, be rebuilt as a floating hotel, motel, conference center, missionary ship and even ceremoniously return to New York on 4 July 1976, the American Bicentennial. The Government had studies done about reviving her, but for military purposes, either as a big troopship or, more likely, as a hospital ship. But nothing came to pass. She was soon offered for sale and finally purchased, in 1980, by Seattle-based real estate developer Richard Hadley. Briefly dry-docked at Norfolk prior to the final transfer, Hadley formed US Cruises with the intent of reviving the *United States* as a unique condominium-style cruise ship. Rumors peaked, including a full rebuilding of the ship at Hamburg. But further financing was never arranged and all it began to fade as the ship lingered and rusted at that Norfolk pier.

Fred Rodriguez, a former crewmember, has made several visits to the idle superliner since 1980. 'I went aboard at Norfolk in 1980-81 and there were souvenirs and collectibles galore still aboard', he recalled. 'There were even sugar packets marked 'United States Lines' still in the pantries and cupboards. The were also menus, programs, china, silverware and glassware. Twenty or so years later, in 2000, at Philadelphia, I returned and found only the fire hoses to be stamped 'United States Lines'. Of course, the builder's plate was still mounted on the forward superstructure. It remained inspite of everything. I also found the area of my old crew cabin on B Deck forward. It brought back lots of memories. But the *United States* had become a ship of decay and disappearance.'

After Richard Hadley's project for make over the *United States* as a condominium-style cruise ship seemed to be fading, several shipowners took a renewed interest in the liner. 'In 1981-82, I put together a concise and formal proposal to Mr Anthony Chandris to buy the *United States*', said Dimitri Kaparis, the senior naval architect for the Chandris Lines, 'so that we could restore our around-the-world passenger and cruise service with her. Doing an average of 30 knots, I estimated that we could operate 70-day itineraries: Southampton, Piraeus, Suez Canal, Sydney, Honolulu, Los Angeles, Panama Canal, New York and back to Southampton. But Mr Chandris was reluctant. He felt that the fuel consumption would be too high, the air competition too strong and that too few Australians would be coming to the United States and to Europe. My next plan, in 1982-83, was also to buy the *United States*, refit her for 30-knots service, but as a cruise ship. My plans showed that she could run twice-weekly sailings from Miami: three-days to Cancun and Nassau; four days to San Juan and St Thomas.

But, once again, Mr Chandris was reluctant and, with the start of his own lung cancer, more reluctant and cautious' (he died in New York in November 1984).

Despite a lack of money for a full conversion or even any repairs, Richard Hadley retained the *United States* and kept her at Norfolk. She grew shabby, weathered, something of the grand lady falling on hard times. He was always optimistic, however, and occasionally some news release or snippet seemed like the ship would return to active service. In 1986, he had a model made of the liner, but in her revised role as a one-class floating hotel depicted her with a navy-blue hull, white eagles on each side of the bow, the funnel fins extended and the superstructure three decks higher. The forward superstructure was rounded and extended with the kingposts and the hatches gone. The Eagle's Nest Observation Lounge, with huge panoramic windows was placed above the bridge section. An intimate, 50-seat bar was in the white band of the forward funnel. Plans were to install both an elevator and a stairwell inside the stack. Within, according to the revised blueprints, the former cabin-class and tourist-class restaurants were each split in two and recreated as four or five different restaurants: a steak house, a French restaurant and a Polynesian restaurant among them. The first-class dining room would become a combination banquet hall and ballroom and would include a curved grand staircase. The aft cargo hatches were to become a three-level shopping mall. There would also be cabins with private balconies, a health center and one indoor and two outdoor pools. 'There are hundreds of pages of preliminary contracts with the shipyard at Hamburg for this conversion', added Daniel Trachtenberg. 'Many contain initials from staff along with handwritten notes and changes by Hadley himself. By 1988, however, he realized that there was no money or no real hope of even raising money. Hadley and his plans for the ship grew more and more suspect. In the end, she went to the auction block.'

Fred Mayer, who represented so-called Turkish business interests bought the ship at auction in February 1992 He gave a $500,000 down payment on the total purchase price of $2.5 million. That June, the ship departed under tow for Turkey, for a comparatively unknown shipyard at the small port of Tuzla for what was to be finally her conversion to a contemporary, all-one class cruise ship. In August 1993, when I sailed homeward from Southampton to New York on the *Queen Elizabeth 2*, Commodore Robin Woodall spoke enthusiastically to me about refit plans for the *United States* and how, beginning in three years, in the spring of 1996, the two ships would be running together on the North Atlantic. The Turks would still own her, he said, the Swedes (Effjohn International) would manage her and the British (Cunard) would handle the sales and marketing. A year later, with revisions, it was reported that she would be run by Greek-owned Regency Cruises in the highly lucrative, ever-expanding Caribbean trade, but as the Regency dream died in 1995 when the parent company collapsed, the *United States*' fate lingered once more.

'When I visited Istanbul, during a cruise on the *Crystal Harmony*, in August 1994, I called on the small, fifth-floor operations office of Marmara Marine, the ship management company that looked after the idle *United States*. It was difficult to find at first, being tucked away on a very narrow side street and was surrounded by grocery shops and a garage. It was a quiet holiday afternoon and all but one man, who handled incoming phone calls, was at work. The office contained some desks that were crowded together, a few framed portraits of cargo ships on the walls and, resting on a side table, the thick log book that had been created for the transatlantic tow of the *United States* back in the summer of 1992. The ship was then anchored several hours away, at Tuzla, and was looked after by three or four security staff, who often slept aboard and who used a portable stove for cooking. The officer in Istanbul told me very little other than that the ship was otherwise empty, still flew the American flag and was soon to be converted into a cruise ship. He knew that I had written a history of the ship, *The United States: The Story of America's Greatest Ocean Liner*, and so offered to arrange a visit to the ship. He would organize transport to Tuzla on the following morning. The idea, unlikely from the start, was completely declined when he mentioned that there was a launch service each day to the ship, but that often, due to the high winds, the second daily launch was canceled. I might have to spend the night on the ship. An empty, dark, very lonely ocean liner, even the great *United States* was not too appealing.

The planned refit at the shipyards at Tuzla never materialized, mostly because of money problems. There was also trouble with Greenpeace over the asbestos that was aboard. Once, a protest group even painted 'death ship' along the sides. The removal of all asbestos was done at Sevastopol, the naval port in the Ukraine. The ship had been towed there from Tuzla and remained for several months. But like always, there were money problems. Consequently, during this phase, in 1995-96, her lifeboats and davits were removed and sold to pay for the asbestos removal process. The davits and some lifeboats were cut up for scrap; other lifeboats were sold to Ukrainian fishermen. Refit and revival plans never actually came about during the so-called Turkish period and so it was decided, rather surprisingly, to bring the liner back to American waters. There was a revived plan and supposedly stronger possibilities for US-flag cruise service for the ship and so a refit in an American shipyard was thought to be essential. Typically, the whole affair was masked in mystery. There were no press announcements, for example. On 27 June 1996, she was reported to be off Sicily, moving at a scant four knots under a hazy Mediterranean sun. The powerful Dutch ocean-going tug *Smit New York* with fifteen crew members had the former speed queen totally in their charge. A week or so later, a friend reported seeing her from the decks of P&O's *Oriana*. Going in opposite directions, the two ships passed one another in the Straits of Gibraltar.

Two weeks later, on 12 July, she was reported to be headed for Boston, possibly to the former US Navy graving dock, which had been specially reactivated just a few years before for emergency repairs to the *Queen Elizabeth 2*. Previously, Philadelphia was said to have been her destination. But by 26 July, there were problems and lots of accompanying rumors. There was a report that she would be anchored off New York harbor, in the Outer Bay, and then later berthed at either the old Bush Terminal in Brooklyn or at the Military Ocean Terminal in Bayonne. By 19 July, the Boston arrangements had fallen through and Philadelphia was back in the planning. On Sunday afternoon, the 21st, she and the tug were at a near stop off the southern coast of New Jersey and approaching the mouth of the Delaware River. 'The *United States* berthed at ten in the morning, on 24 July, at the Packer Avenue Marine Terminal in Philadelphia', reported keen passenger ship observer Martin Wismer

Fred Mayer, a part owner and chief spokesman, had an early morning meeting with Governor Ridge of Pennsylvania to make arrangements for her refit to a cruise ship at the otherwise closed Philadelphia Navy Yard. The $250 million contract would revive the shipyard as well as the ship and would employ 1,500 shipyard workers for two years. She was already stripped of all her lifeboats and davits. Boston did not materialize due to problems with height restrictions [including for air routes in and out of Logan International Airport] and a wreck blocking access to the old Navy graving dock.

'I was struck by the immenseness of the *United States'*, said another fan of the ship, Larry A. Hansen, 'and also the fact that the ship was positioned so close to the Walt Whitman Bridge. You could almost step off the bridge and onto the top of the forward funnel. There were a number of other people gazing at her from the bridge walkway. One man had been a steward aboard her and two couples had traveled on her. For all the years of neglect, however, there is still a majestic quality to the *United States*. Now, she is faded glory. This magnificent ship certainly deserves a better ending.'

By the fall of 1996, Charleston, Savannah and Jacksonville were said to be interested if and when the ship was refitted, but as a combination hotel-convention center-museum. San Francisco and New Orleans were later mentioned as well. Another ocean liner enthusiast, engineer Tom Cangialosi, visited the ship several times in 1997. 'She was moved to Pier 96, at the foot of Ogden Avenue in Philadelphia, early last December', he reported. 'Otherwise, she sat in sad majesty: silent and lifeless. On the outside, there was very little rigging between those two great funnels. All the lifeboats, once numbering twenty-four in all, and the davits were gone. Some of the portholes and promenade windows were smashed. Of course, there was lots of rust and peeling paint.' With a powerful flashlight in hand, Cangialosi toured the darkened interiors as well. 'She was actually very tidy on the inside', he said in an interview the following fall. 'She had been swept clean here at Philadelphia. But all else was gone. There was very little trace of yesterday, the glamor years, of that most impeccable ship afloat. She was now like a vast cavern in places. The major partitions have gone and so have all the cabins. You could barely identify any of the old public rooms. Only a few stairwells were in tact. I did see a few unattached sinks, one bathtub down on C Deck, the telephone switchboard under a tarp and a few pieces of furniture. I could sense the downward pitch in the main theater. Eisenhower had watched *The Longest Day* in that very room. The theater floor was still all blue, but the control room was dark and empty. I spotted a calendar for 1966. On each deck, there was still some of the black linoleum bearing the appropriate markings: A Deck, B Deck, C Deck. C Deck was the only entry to the ship and it was very easy to get lost once you are aboard. She was very, very dark in places. There was also a sickly sweet smell throughout the ship, a blend of mould and lingering bunker oil. The mechanical areas were pitch dark except for a single, lighted bulb operating from a small portable generator, a concession to safety ordered by the Philadelphia Fire Department. She was also completely still, not a sound anywhere onboard. There was slight motion, however, when a tug or a barge passed. That was the only sign of any life in the great *United States*. The only ventilation on board to the vast complex of darkened decks, passageways and stairwells was through the broken Promenade Deck windows. The four props rested on the aft decks and the stern railing had been badly smashed (done in Turkey when one of the props was being lifted aboard). Old, unhinged doors also filled the open, aft decks. On the inside, there were scribblings and chalk marks on the bare walls made by the ship's construction crews back in 1951-52.'

Alan Zamchick was another visitor to the idle ship, but on an autumn day in 1997. 'My first sight of her was crossing the Franklin Street Bridge. She still looked impressive, majestic, very powerful', he recalled. 'She looked like she wanted to get away and sail. She seemed to be straining at the dock. Of course, she retained that perfect balance: a low superstructure and two huge funnels. But otherwise, she looked sad, very sad. Paint was peeling everywhere, like a snake shedding its skin. There were broken portholes and windows. It was all sorry neglect. A beautiful icon of the 1950s seemed to have taken on the confusion and disorder of the 1960s and 1970s. She was the dream ship of an era. But she was now an old lady, a gracious lady, that had seen better days. Now, it was all nostalgia, those bygone days on the Atlantic. Even her owner at the time was uninterested. In a flash, you thought it might be better to scrap or even sink her. But she should be kept as a museum, a great testament to another time. The interior grandness is completely destroyed, of course. She has been completely gutted and stripped. The Duck Suite doesn't have ducks anymore!'

The Turks, namely Marmara Marine, and still outwardly headed by Fred Mayer, owned the ship until November 1997. At that time, the ship was seized by US marshals since the balance of $2 million had not been paid since the June 1992 auction at Norfolk. Only $500,000 had been transferred. Businessman Robert Cantor was the only bidder in the 1997 auction. His bid was $6 million and so he became the new owner. Actually, Cantor and Mayer were friends, having met some years before when their yachts were anchored together in Turkey. Cantor, a New Jersey-based businessman, is said to have made a fortune in real estate, in housing and in warehousing. Mayer convinced Cantor to become an investor in what was then called the SS *United States* Project. But by 2001, Cantor was asking as much as $35 million for the ship, a figure said to be based on his investment, the $1,000-a-day docking fees over five years and a rumored $1 million in annual insurance. Below all others, the high selling price has kept scrap merchants away from the ship. They have offered $3.4-$4 million in recent years and find her attractive since she is certifiably asbestos-free. Cantor had reportedly appointed numerous brokers, some real, but many self-styled, who might sell the ship. He supposedly offered them 10 per cent of the purchase price, which would be $3.5 million if the $35 million price tag was realized.

'Unfortunately, this has all attracted many potential buyers, middlemen, schemers, dreamers and many less than scrupulous to all of this', Daniel Trachtenberg added, 'Consequently, no one ship has had a more uncertain afterlife or been the subject of more rumor, scheme and mislaid plans. The rumors continued, of course. The summer of 1999 was especially plentiful with ideas. That July, there were said to be plans to move her from her costly Philadelphia berth to a less expensive dock. New York was again high on the list. The Brooklyn Navy Yard or Port Authority Pier 1 at the foot of Fulton Street in Brooklyn Heights were said to be the strong possibilities. Also back in the rumor mill were plans to remake the superliner, said to be for sale for an astronomical $33 million (this against her estimated scrap value of $2 million), into a large gambling casino with huge cuts made along her sides for garages. Las Vegas interests were said to be studying plans and were keen on New York as a home base. 'Brooklyn authorities were interested at the time, but only if the ship had a commercial interest, say as a hotel or convention center', noted Daniel Trachtenberg, then the vice-president of the SS *United States* Foundation, a volunteer group that wanted to see the ship saved, but which often acted on behalf of the ship's owner.

The Brooklyn Navy Yard site would have required taking off the two mammoth funnels, which itself would have cost between $200,000 and $300,000, to clear the Brooklyn and the Manhattan Bridges along the East River. The stacks would have been placed on a barge, floated in separately and then reattached. She would have been docked at the Navy's old dry docks, either Number 5 or 6. The Federal Government was interested in seeing the yard redeveloped, but in a positive way. They even sent a team out to the *Queen Mary* at Long Beach to determine feasibility and viability. Of course, the Fulton Street berth would have been ideal as it was just across from the South Street Seaport. The *United States* would have been moored lengthwise and would have made a wonderful sight, both in day and at night. Another notation was added to the ship's history earlier that same summer. Over the Fourth-of-July weekend, her funnels, wheelhouse windows and crow's nest were lighted for the first time in over thirty years, since she was laid up at Newport News in November 1969. On the 2nd, the lights were on for just a few minutes before the portable generators that had been brought aboard failed. On the 3rd, the lights blazed in the Philadelphia night from 9 o'clock until well into the next morning. On the 4th, they were operative only for a short time, at sunset.

Robert Wogan, a freelance artist with a specialty in obsolete machinery, created and underwrote the project. He had just discovered the ship's location on the Internet weeks before and had remembered the *United States* from a childhood visit at New York. He contacted the Cantor organization as well as the SS *United States* Foundation and was given permission to light the ship. 'It cost about $9,000 to rent several generators and 70lb floodlights', said Trachtenberg, who assisted Robert and his team. 'The lights had to be hauled to the top decks while cables and thick wires from the generators ran from the dockside. It was a good thing for Independence Day, but it was only covered in the local papers. The stacks could be seen for miles around and the fireworks across in Camden, New Jersey, created an overall great effect. The ship looked hauntingly majestic. All you needed was to have some windows and portholes lighted as well and it might have been a normal night-time sailing scene from her earlier days. The two funnels actually looked quite good. But he did not want them painted. He wanted them exposed, as it was.'

'Within, the *United States* was quiet, dark and totally stripped', explained Trachtenberg, who visited the vessel several dozen times by 1999. 'It is very easy to get lost once onboard. Some stairwells just end. You always need a flashlight. There is still a little oil onboard (from 1969) and it has been leaking, but it is more like tar because of its age. Some openings on the ship had to be re-secured. And rainwater accumulates in some internal areas, sometimes in the middle of the old passenger decks. Some water stays for long periods and consequently there is considerable rusting. The owners do minimal maintenance, even some occasional light cleaning. The ship still moans and creaks at times. Frank Braynard once told me, ships talk to you and the *United States* is one of them.'

But by 1999 and after three years since her arrival, public interest, at least at Philadelphia, had lessened according to Trachtenberg. 'After she first arrived in the summer of 1996, people even jumped over the fence to get close to the ship

Idle and rusting at Norfolk in a view from June 1979. (Author's Collection)

and some even cut the barbed wire. Some arrived by cabin cruiser and even tried to climb the dangling anchor chain. Locals often ask if she had sunk and then been salvaged because of her poor condition. They sometimes compared her to the *Titanic*.'

'The summer of 1999 brought about a slightly different proposal and might have seen the ship bought to New York, in fact to former Pier 84, along Luxury Liner Row. We met with representatives, who claimed to be from a major hospital. Their plan was to turn the *United States* into a kidney treatment and research center', Trachtenberg explained. 'They said it would be cheaper to convert the ship than construct a new building. They wanted it to be operational by the summer of 2000 and even went so far as to plan to have President Clinton open it. It was to be a combined effort between the hospital itself and financial investors, and the ship was to be berthed at West 44 Street, just across from the USS *Intrepid* Museum. But in time, after meetings, discussions, even site inspections, it all came to nothing. There were even meetings with the *Intrepid* Museum people. In the end, it faded quickly. Our last phone calls went unanswered.'

'Months later, by the fall of 1999, yet another project was brewing, in fact at its peak. New York-based Original Ventures Incorporated had wanted to use the *United States* as a New York hotel since her return from Turkey in 1996. This company had been interested in a hotel project at the New York Coliseum at Columbus Circle, but when that failed they thought of the ship', said Trachtenberg. 'Their office was filled with artist renderings and even some models of their many proposals: hotels, themed shopping malls and even the likes of indoor ski slopes. They saw the *United States* as a period-piece hotel with a museum onboard as well. It was called Flotel United States and a short video was made for presentation purposes. The SS *United States* Foundation would run the museum portion. Half would be devoted to ocean liner history, the other half to the Port of New York's history. Discussions with New York City officials were soon pre-empted, however, by City Hall's interest in other projects such as a West Side sports stadium and waterfront parklands. Original Ventures had first eyed Pier 76, a former United States Lines cargo terminal, at West 36 Street, which they planned to extend by 300ft to accommodate the 990ft liner', said Trachtenberg.

'There was to be a bridge across Twelfth Avenue to the Javits Convention Center and there was to be rooftop parking on Pier 76. The Convention Center was never directly interested in the ship, but they were excited that the project could increase their business as well as possibly breathe new life into the west side of Manhattan. But in the end, city officials preferred Pier 94, a former Cunard freighter berth, because of the planned Hudson River Park, which will extend from the Chelsea Piers to the *Intrepid* Museum. They said that Pier 76 is to be removed and furthermore that a big liner would interfere with the overall Hudson River view. Original Ventures grew less interested in Pier 94. They especially liked the Javits Center connection. But by February 2001, even the Pier 94 scheme was dead. There had been a rumor that the J.P. Morgan Company would finance up to $200 million for a Hudson River pier project for the *United States*, but actually much more would be needed. By 2006, as the decay at Philadelphia deepened and other plans had long faded, Miami-based Norwegian Cruise Lines, then developing a US-flag cruise division in Hawaii, was said to have purchased *United States* and were planning to revive her for cruising. Timed press releases were somewhat encouraging, but again nothing came to pass. By late 2008, and with their US-flag cruise operation much diminished and reduced, and the worldwide economic slump intensifying, any future for the ship with Norwegian Cruise Lines seemed most unlikely.

As this book goes to press in fall 2009, not a single fact, or even a snippet of fresh news about the *United States* has come forth. Quietly, she sits at her Philadelphia pier. But the stage setting had changed somewhat. The economic downturn in the USA as well as the rest of the world has prompted bankruptcies, closures, cuts, downsizing, some major lay-offs. The multi-billion dollar international cruise industry, with an average of two new ships per month coming on line, suddenly seemed almost top heavy. Cruise lines were having to discount fares to fill their ships, many of them in the size category with as many as 6,000 berths, by as much as 75 per cent. Clearly, there was no need to rebuild a ship nearing 60 such as the *United States* and even floating hotels seemed as unlikely. At least three recent proposals for aged passenger ships fell by the wayside. Museum ships seemed equally as unlikely. The fate of the *United States* has become more obvious. Indeed, the *United States* served a very great purpose. She easily deserved her title: America's finest liner. There was no ship quite like her. She was a floating showcase of national brilliance. She set records, lured passengers, made money and triumphantly carried the red, white and blue overseas. Along with the likes of the *Queen Mary*, *Queen Elizabeth* and *France*, the Atlantic liner became the casualty of a newer, expanding technology: commercial aviation and, in particular, the big jets. The era of the transatlantic passenger ship had passed. Sadly, nothing ever came of the *United States* other than lay-up, neglect, pages of schemes and proposals. Unquestionably, she deserves better, a concluding chapter, that last paragraph in her story. But now, this book is meant as a tribute to that finest of ships, a grand salute and perhaps even adds something to her story. Hail to the SS *United States*!

Left: United States is moved for the first time in over ten years, to the Norshipco Shipyard at Norfolk in May 1980 for hull inspection. (Norshipco)

Right: The great liner in dry dock at Norfolk. (Norshipco)

Above left: Growth on the two starboard propellers as seen while in dry dock at Norfolk. (Norshipco)

Above right: The long-neglected propellers seen when the ship was placed in dry dock in May 1980. (Norshipco)

Left: During the auctions and other sales of her fittings in the early 1980s, even the whistles from the funnels were sold off to raise much needed cash. (Author's Collection)

Right: Although silent and empty, the *United States* is floodlit in this scene at a Norfolk shipyard. (Norshipco)

Left: Seen from decks of the missionary ship *Anastasis*, also at Norfolk and in November 1989. (Author's Collection)

Right: A stern view at Norfolk dated November 1989. (Author's Collection)

Above: The funnels of the *United States* and the sports deck. (J&C McCutcheon Collection)

Right: The great bow, also from 1989. (Author's Collection)

Below: The still elegant lines of the neatly placed promenade windows. (Author's Collection)

In November 1989, entry to the otherwise silent, empty ship was through a single gangway that was looked after by two custodians. (Author's Collection)

The stern section with her homeport still showing as New York. (Author's Collection)

Above: A pleasant, congenial dining saloon adds much to the enjoyment of any meal. The walls of the first-class Dining Saloon are of an off-white while the aluminum leaf is glazed gold and the lighting indirect. A far cry from 1989. (J&C McCutcheon Collection)

Right: Well faded and long discolored, the twin funnels as seen from the stern. (Author's Collection)

Below: Desolate, lonely and in disarray, the first-class Dining Room as seen in November 1989. (Author's Collection)

Left: Part of the enclosed promenade was littered with the steel coils from stateroom bed springs. (Author's Collection)

Below: The emptiness of the sitting room of the famed Duck Suite. (Author's Collection)

The desolation of the public rooms. (Author's Collection)

Peeling paint along the starboard promenade windows.
(Author's Collection)

Above left: At anchor at Tuzla in Turkey in July 1992. (Steffen Weirauch)

Above right: Return to US waters, to Philadelphia, in this view dated 27 July 1996. (Peter Knego Collection)

Left: Under the care of a sea-going tug, the *United States* departs from Norfolk bound for Turkey in 1992. (Backus Aerial Photography)

Above: Moored beneath the Walt Whitman Bridge at Philadelphia in July 1996. (Derek Bergl)

Above right: The great stacks, even if faded and discolored, added to the cityscape. (Author's Collection)

Below: The builder's plate aboard the idle, neglected liner. (Author's Collection

Below right: Once filled with happy passengers, the empty first-class Dining Room. (Captain Robert Russell Collection)

UNITED STATES

DESIGNERS
GIBBS AND COX, INC.

BUILDERS
1952   NEWPORT NEWS № 488
SHIPBUILDING AND DRY DOCK CO.

MARITIME COMMISSION № 2917

The badly neglected tourist-class Smoking Room as seen in
November 1997. (Peter Knego Collection)

The starboard enclosed Promenade Deck. (Robert Russell
Collection)

Above: Her lifeboats and their davits are gone, as clearly seen in this view. (Author's Collection)

Above right: The forward superstructure. (Captain Robert Russell Collection)

Right: Another view of the forward superstructure. (Peter Knego Collection)

Cargo hatch number one. (Captain Robert Russell Collection)

The stern section. (Captain Robert Russell Collection)

Left: Cargo hatch number two. (Captain Robert Russell Collection)

Right: The starboard aft sports deck. (Captain Robert Russell Collection)

Above left: Peeling paint on the otherwise distinctive funnel. (Author's Collection)

Above right: The once gleaming radar mast atop the bridge section. (Author's Collection)

Above: The promenade deck windows and the funnel above. (Author's Collection)

Right: The two great funnels. (Author's Collection)

Below: Another view of those winged stacks. (Author's Collection)

The ship retains great presence as seen in this view. (John McFarlane Collection)

At Philadelphia in 2006. (John McFarlane Collection)

Above: A close-up of the bridge section and forward funnel. (John McFarlane Collection)

Right: The starboard bow section. (John McFarlane Collection)

Below: Her bow is marked with the scars of tow ropes but the SS *United States* still looks majestic even in lay up. (John McFarlane Collection)

BIBLIOGRAPHY

Braynard, Frank O.   *By Their Works Ye Shall Know Them*, New York: Gibbs & Cox, 1968.

Miller, William H.   *Passenger Liners American Style*, London: Carmania Press Ltd, 1999.

Picture History of American Passenger Ships, Mineola, New York: Dover Publications Inc.

Picture History of the SS United States, Mineola, New York: Dover Publications Inc., 2003.

SS United States: The History of America's Greatest Liner, Sparkford, England: Patrick Stephens Ltd, 1991.

Lost in a neglected limbo for forty years, the *United States* at Philadelphia. (Author's Collection)